WHEN ɪɴ ROME

• • • • • • • • • • • •

THE HUMORISTS'
GUIDE TO ITALY

Other Humorists' Guides

WHEN IN ROME

· · · · · · · · · · · · · ·

THE HUMORISTS' GUIDE TO ITALY

Edited by Robert Wechsler

CATBIRD PRESS

CATBIRD PRESS
44 North Sixth Avenue
Highland Park, NJ 08904
201-572-0816

Distributed to the trade by Independent Publishers Group

The Humorists' Guides are available at special bulk-purchase
discounts for promotions, premiums, and fund-raising.
For details, contact Catbird Press at the above address.

The publisher wishes to acknowledge permission to include
in this book copyright material as follows:

LUDWIG BEMELMANS: "The Isle of Capri": Copyright 1953 Ludwig Bemelmans; illustration from *Italian Holiday*: Copyright 1961 Ludwig Bemelmans. Both reprinted by permission of International Creative
Management, Inc. ACKNOWLEDGMENTS are continued at the back of
the book.

CONTENTS

INTRODUCTION

TRAVEL GUIDES ARE WHAT YOU READ when you want to know where to stay and what to see and where to eat and what to do about such things as visas and hotels and shopping. This is not that sort of guide.

Humorists don't care how much you'll have to spend to go in style—or without it. They know you'll spend more than you expected, that you'll squabble about expenses, about buying this trinket or that pair of gloves, but that the experience will be priceless no matter how many zillions of liras pass through your wallet or purse.

So forget everything you've ever thought about guidebooks. The advice here is much simpler: relax and enjoy. Remember: it's your vacation—holiday time—so don't annoy yourself about the prices or the services or the purse-snatchers. Well, if you have to worry about something, go ahead and worry about the purse-snatchers, but you'd do better to keep your valuables in your pockets.

Although we go to Italy to see the Michelangelos and Leonardos, what we see more of, and what humorists can never get enough of, are the Georgios and Giovannis, the Marias and Antonias, not to mention our fellow Johns and Marys. Humor is about people, about how they react to all those things the travel guides describe, as well as how they react to each other. Humor couldn't care less about *what* will serve us best; it prefers to look at *who* will manage not to. It's interested not in where we set down our bags, but in the baggage we all carry with us: awe

1

and delight, playfulness and absurdity, dreams and nightmares, myths and stereotypes, platitudes and pretensions, expectations and obsessions, anger and fear and love.

Yes, *When in Rome* is more than just another pretty guidebook. Behind that sparkling veneer is a serious humor anthology, a treasury of the best humorous writing about traveling in Italy, by humorists who travel and travel writers who have a sense of humor. Among the selections are many that are simply fun or silly or nonsensical, many that make unusual or ironic observations, many that satire or parody or find some other way to poke fun at, many that take delight in what they see, and some that do all of these at once. Although many of the selections are vintage, little of the humor here is about the way things used to be; it's too easy to laugh at our fathers and grandmothers. This is a book about the ways things are and will, most likely, be.

There are unknown finds in *When in Rome,* such as Anthony Thorne's "Beautifully Done," as well as classics of the genre, such as Mark Twain's "The Old Masters." Several of the greatest English-speaking humorists are represented in these pages. Americans will recognize the names of Roy Blount, Jr., Art Buchwald, Irvin S. Cobb, S.J. Perelman, Will Rogers, Mark Twain, and Alexander Woollcott. Britons will recognize the names of Alan Brien, Alan Coren, Edward Lear, and George Mikes.

When in Rome also includes selections from the work of travel writers, many of whom are best known for their other works, mostly novels. People like Ludwig Bemelmans, Charles Dickens, Donald Hall, Henry James, William Dean Howells, Emily Kimbrough, D. H. Lawrence, Stephen Longstreet, Aubrey Menen, H. V. Morton, and Sean O'Faolain.

And we can't forget the cartoonists and illustrators. Few of them are household names; only Rube Goldberg would fit that bill. One is also represented by his prose, Ludwig Bemelmans, and the others' work can be found in such publications as *Punch, The New Yorker,* and *The Wall Street Journal.*

Well, that's enough names. Now you won't have to read the table of contents. Enjoy the book—in sips, gulps, and guzzles, however you like—and let me thank all the people who helped make *When in Rome* possible, particularly the all-too-forgotten souls who work in the permissions departments of publishing houses; the families of the authors; their literary agents; and, most of all, those humorists who stubbornly point their mighty pens at windmills and the like. Special thanks go to Mircea Vasiliu, whose drawing graces the cover; to Pat Lesnefsky, who took a pile of xeroxed pieces and managed to fit them all on a single diskette; to Len Ringel and Stacy Wszola, who designed and laid out the cover; to Axiom Design Systems in New York City, which set the type; to R. R. Donnelley & Sons in Crawfordsville, Indiana, which printed and bound the copy you're reading; and, last but hardly least, to any reader who gives another copy of this book as a present and thereby keeps the Catbird in seed.

By the way, occasionally you will see a * * * in the middle of a selection. This means that some irrelevant text was left out, either about something other than Italy or about something that means nothing today.

Mark Twain
Learning Italian

❧Preparations

❧*Italy. How does one prepare for a country like Italy? Packing is itself such a crisis, you might find yourself gesturing and talking just as fast and heartily as an Italian. T-shirts and shorts for the heat of the southern countryside, the most fashionable togs we own for the northern cities, comfortable shoes for all the museums and churches, swimming suits for the Italian Riviera (...and how little do they really wear?), boots in honor of the peninsula's shape, warm sweaters for the northern lakes, and long underwear for the Alps? Who could ever carry that much luggage! And how could you ever carry home all the things you want to buy there? No, just forget it. It's impossible to pack for Italy.*

And it's equally impossible to prepare yourself emotionally for what you're about to see. Heights of modernity glaring across at heights of classicism, heights of medievalism, and heights of Renaissance. It's enough to make you dizzy. And then the myths! The Roman gods and the Roman empire, the Borgias and the popes, Botticelli and Michelangelo, Garibaldi and Mussolini, Milan and Palermo. To many who know Italy only from novels and films, as well as to Alan Coren, the editor of Britain's top humor magazine Punch, *Palermo seems to be the capital of Italy and the center of its most compelling mythology.*

Alan Coren
Italy 1980

The People
The median Italian, according to the latest figures of
the Coren Intelligence Unit, is a cowardly baritone who
consumes 78.3 kilometres of carbohydrates a month and
drives about in a car slightly smaller than he is, looking
for a divorce. He is governed by a stable conservative
government, called the Mafia, who operate an efficient
police force, called the Mafia, which is the official arm of
the judiciary, called the Mafia. The Italians are an extremely cultivated folk, and will often walk miles to sell a
tourist a copy of the Sistine Chapel ceiling made entirely
from sea-shells. They invented the mandoline, a kind of
boudoir banjo shaped like a woman's bottom, not
surprisingly.

The Land
Italy is boot-shaped, for reasons lost in the mists of
geology. The South is essentially agricultural, and ad-
ministered by local land authorities, called the Mafia; the
North is industrial, and run by tightly interlocked cor-
porations, called the Mafia. The largest Italian city is New
York, and is linked to the mainland by a highly special-
ised and efficient communications system, called the
Mafia.

The History
Italy was originally called Rome, which came to hold
power over Europe by moving into new areas every week
or so and threatening to lean on them if they did not fork
out tithe (L. *protectio*). It was run by a series of Caesars
(Eduardus Gaius Robinsonius, Georgius Raftus, Paulus
Munius, etc.) who held sway until the Renaissance, when
Leonardo invented the tank and the aeroplane, and thus

ushered in modern Italy (in World War II, the Italians, ever brilliant, possessed the only tank with a reverse gear). In the 1920s, the Caesars reasserted themselves in their two main linear branches, the Caponi and the Mussolini, whose symbol was the fasces, which signified "United We Stand," but they didn't.

❧*Although most of us don't learn Italian in school, it's one of those languages it seems so easy to speak. Just add a vowel to the end of every word and put to work parts of your body you never thought could speak a single syllable. A phrasebook, a tape, maybe even a few lessons might just let you feel you can get by. Just like* uno, due, tre. *And even if you don't say the right words, or say them right, it'll sound just fine to your ear, and to your friends'.*

To prepare yourself for the agonies and ecstasies of trying to speak Italian, here are the great contemporary American travel humorist—not to mention all-around funny guy—Roy Blount, Jr. on what just a few Italian lessons can do for your self-confidence, travel writer John Gibbons on the Italian phrasebook, Mark Twain on the one-word-a-day-method, and an anecdote by the classic humorist George Ade, as told to his peer Irvin S. Cobb. Finally, for those who have no intention of learning a single word of Italian except for non capisco, *the Czechoslovak travel writer, novelist, and playwright Karel Capek has a few soothing words.*

Roy Blount, Jr.
Italian Wasn't Learned in a Day 1988

"Per favore, ci riservi un tavolo per due per le due."

THIS WAS ME SPEAKING! Reserving a table for two for two o'clock at Sabatini I, a restaurant in Rome. Over the Italian telephone, coolly. Italian wouldn't melt in my mouth. And then the man who had answered the phone said, in his native tongue (my translation):

"Men?"

Why would he ask that? As a matter of fact, my twosome was mixed. What business of his was it whether... And what made him think he ought to check? Was it something I said? My thoughts sped like wildfire....

No, that's *spread* like wildfire, isn't it? The deeper I get into Italian, the more my English suffers. My thoughts sped, like ... something fast, back over what I had said.

Un tavolo. I knew that was right. Unless—was there some word that sounded a lot like *tavolo* that had non-heterosexual connotations? And what if there were? What was the securely but uninvidiously straight response here, in Italian? How would I know? I'd had only five and a quarter hours of Italian, not counting lunch. And lunch had not been all that Italian because it was included in the $387.06 I'd paid for a one-day crash course in Italian at Berlitz in midtown Manhattan, and all the Italian restaurants around there were expensive, so my instructor and I had eaten at La Bonne Soupe.

But my studies lay five days in the past. Now I was in Rome, on the firing line, and ... wait. How could you conduct any sort of restaurant business by telephone if there were a word with nonheterosexual connotations that sounded like the word for "table?"

Maybe the problem lay in the *dues*. (If my mastery of the language were greater, I sensed quickly, I might be able to make a joke about having paid my *dues*, but I had neither time nor Italian enough for that now.) Was it possible I had given the impression that I was reserving a table for two people names Dewey and Dewey, the latter of them referred to for some reason as *the* Dewey?

No. Wait. The word for "man" in Italian was *uomo* (no connotations), the plural was *uomini*. What the man taking reservations had said was *"Signori?"* Which meant "Gentlemen?"

What he really wanted to know, then, was whether Dewey and *the* Dewey were of the right class. The nerve!, *(Il nervo!)* Perhaps my Italian was not on a par with that of some vestigial patrician whose ancestors had scattered like rabbits *(conigli)* at the first hint of Visigoths, but where did this guy get off...?

"Americano?" he said then.

Oh ho, I thought to myself (in English, because I'd had only the one day's immersion in Italian). Restaurants in Rome had a quota on Americans named Dewey. I was angry—but how to express it?

"Si..." I said, temporizing, sticking to basic vocabulary, struggling to put some kind of spin on the word that would sound like ... some kind of spin.

Then he said a thing that hurt my feelings. "Are you talking?" he said. In English.

And then, as I groped for a suitably stiff reply to this impertinent question, something else hit me. What he must have said to begin with was not *"Signori?"* but *"Signore...?"* as in "Mister...?" He must simply have wanted to know what my last name was so he could book the reservation. Was it too late to answer that question now? Unfortunately, my name—four consonants surrounding one sluggish, questionable vowel sound—does not sound like anything at all in Italian.

I decided to deal with the most recent question. *"Si..."* I said. Fighting for time.

Then it occurred to me that perhaps *"Signore?"* had just meant "Sir?" But I couldn't pause to mull that over because it would require several more split seconds of silence and I had just said yes, I was talking.

"...in inglese?" he asked. Which means, "in English?"

"No," I said, in Italian. But how do you say "I am speaking in Italian" in Italian? *Io parlo italiano* means "I speak Italian," which wasn't strictly true, as I had had only the seven lessons plus lunch.

"In English or Italian, are you talking or are you not talking? Come on man, wake up," he said. In English. I won't be spoken to like that. Not in my own first language. I hung up.

"Are you talking?" indeed! Easy for him to talk. He is a person who answers the telephone in Italian for a living. Whereas I...

When my one-day course at Berlitz began, I couldn't speak more than a handful of words in Italian. When it ended, I couldn't speak more than a handful of words in English, either.

But that was fatigue. A person would feel that way after being immersed all day in anything—water, for instance. I took seven 45-minute classes, and French lunch, in Italian. And I got to where I was speaking up to three sentences at a stretch! If you count *"No"* as a sentence. For example: *"Sono io la signora Dussi? No. Io sono il signor Blount."*

I spent a whole day speaking scarcely a word of English, except *sottovoce*. (The walls—*lepareti*—had ears. My several instructors would point to the walls and whisper, "They are listening." That is, the school's management was monitoring, making sure we were confining ourselves to Italian. Confining ourselves! To the least pinched, at least *sentimento*-wise, of tongues!)

There my instructors and I were, tearing off great chunks of Italian, all about doors and doctors and hats *(cappelli)*. Pictures were held up. Fingers were pointed. Hand gestures were made. Verbs and conjunctions were rendered inferable. (*E* is "and," and *è* is "is.") And at one point Signora Dussi—the only one of my teachers whose name I got entirely straight—said to me, *"Bravissimo!"*

Which means "Bravo very much."

Let me say that I majored in English for four years of college and one of graduate school. And in that entire time no teacher every said to me, *"Bravissimo!"* Of course I never came up with anything in English that sounded as good as this:

"L'Arno non è una strada e non è una città."

Which is pronounced:

"Larno known eh oona strada ay known eh oona cheetah."

And which means: "The Arno is not a street and is not a city."

And which is the closest I can come, in Italian, to "I know a little place called doo-wah-diddy. It ain't no town and it ain't no city."

Imagine my being able to come that close to something that hip in Italian! I can even tell you what the Arno is. *È un lungo fiume.*

What a fine language Italian is in many ways. As I understand it, every little syllable is pronounced, wholeheartedly. Which I think is something the French ought to look into. The French, if you ask me, take undue advantage of the fact that so much of their language amounts to elaborate but probably indistinguishable variations on *ong.* I took French in high school and college, but in my experience if you try to speak it to a Frenchman whom you are not paying anything or whom you have already paid, he will look at you as if you are not speaking anything at all.

11

Whereas my day's worth of Berlitz Italian, supplemented by a phrase book, enabled me to ask a Roman waiter, *"Perchè non ci sono carciofi?"* And although he was already pocketing the tip, and I am not at all sure the *ci* was in the right place, he answered at some length and I could sort of follow him. There were no artichokes because the weather was not right, there had not been enough water. From what I gather, he was even telling the truth. An Italian, speaking to me with perfect candor in Italian.

"Grazie," I said, and I meant it.

On the other hand, as we have seen, there was my experience with the man who answered the phone at Sabatini I. So I am not going to fall head over heels into Italian.

I have a pretty good thing going with American English. It keeps food in my mouth. Is that right? That can't be right. It keeps food on the table. That doesn't seem quite right either. But when it comes to American English, I am constantly aware that I never quite know what I am saying.

One night in Rome, in the American bar of the Hotel de la Ville, I spoke, in English, with a Japanese businessman about America. He was from Hiroshima, but he said he didn't hold that against me. He said in fact he was glad that Americans had occupied Japan because his people had learned much from our culture. However, he said, there was one thing about Americans ... he searched for an example.

A colleague of his, he said, had been in America. Had penetrated so far as Ohio. And there, in a private home, this colleague "was served a sandwich of penis butter. Penis butter? Penis butter. I think it is an example of Protestantism and capitalism."

"Ah," I said. I looked at him, and nodded. And I thought to myself (in English): I have been speaking

Italian. And people have been looking at me, and nodding.

John Gibbons
You Know the Sort of Book 1932

DOWNSTAIRS AN OLD WOMAN had come in, and as I pointed to my mouth with my usual "*Mangiare*" she threw some twigs on to the little kitchen grate and began to make welcome preparations for a meal. Details, of course, you leave to your hostess, for the only time that I had tried my Italian for suggestions I came to awful grief. "Eggs," I had asked for (*uove* is the word), and then, as I hadn't known what else to say, I got the beastly things raw. The Italians sometimes take them that way, cracking them ever so delicately, and pouring the whole concern right down their throats. But I hadn't had the knack of it, and made a most filthy mess. So after that I used to leave well enough alone. You would never have thought it from the look of the kitchen-sitting-room, but this particular woman turned out an admirable meal of several courses. And all within minutes.

Then, after I had eaten it, there seemed nothing else particular to do just then. Later, perhaps, a promenade round the place, but not at present. Not under that sun. And so I loafed about the single room, smoking cigarettes and playing with the baby and trying to talk to the girl. I tried her once or twice with bits from my phrase-book, but pronounce them how I would, the business was hopeless. Till in disgust I threw the thing down on the table. She picked it up in a minute, and then, as the Italian dawned upon her, she went thoroughly into the matter. And a quarter of an hour later that child of fourteen or so had me learning Italian under her able tuition. She would give me a phrase from the book, and then I should have to say it over and over again until I got it to her liking. And by and by she had in all her friends to listen to me, till the little room was crowded. Indeed, before I had finished I was reading through the window to people collected in the *piazza* below.

You know the sort of book, and how the traveller it is written for starts out in fine form. "Porter, I have eight packages here in the carriage, and there are sixteen more in the guard's van. Get them out at once and there will be a handsome tip for you." (Not a word about the other poor beggars, all anxious for their luggage!) And then, by and by, the selfish brute gets into difficulties and loses most of his twenty-four packages, and it is "Cabman, drive me at once to the police station. At once, I say." There were lots of fruity bits like that in the thing. There was one piece I was awfully good at. "Porter," it was called, "is there a lift in this hotel?" Because there wasn't, you see. There was a porch place downstairs where some chickens lived till they were wanted, there was the kitchen part above that, and then, further up still, was the floor where we slept. It was a very friendly hotel indeed. But there was certainly no lift. Another passage for which I actually got an encore began: "Cabman, you have not given me the correct change." And after the opening line it went into variations. "Cabman, you have given me too little change," and "Cabman, you have given me too much change." It was the "too much change" part that tickled the popular fancy.

But I think my very best bit was the "Cabman, drive me at once to the British Consulate" one. Of course there is not much in it simply in reading, but if you could only have seen the place, with about two hundred miles of sheer savage wilderness all round it, and the one coach from rail-head, fifty miles away to the south, not due till next day, the point might have struck you better. Any amount of snow on the mountains towering round the little town, and perfectly real wolves; but no cabman, and no British consulate.

Irvin S. Cobb
A Terrible Tragedy 1925

GEORGE ADE ALWAYS CLAIMED that it happened to a friend of his. Personally, I believe he
made it up. Be that as it may, it's a good story.

Ade's suppositious friend was traveling through Italy.
He dined one night at a café in Naples. The behavior of
two Italian gentlemen at an adjacent table interested him
deeply. What they said made no difference to him, as he
spoke no Italian, but the pantomime between them held
his attention. I can well understand that. To me, Italian
has always seemed not so much a language as a calisthenic exercise. In other words, if the speaker's hands
were tied and his shoulders were paralyzed, I'm sure he
couldn't utter a sound.

After watching the nearby pair for some time, the
Yankee beckoned to the head-waiter to draw nigh. The
head-waiter was Swiss and knew half a dozen tongues,
including English.

"You've been standing just behind the couple at the
next table," said the American; "probably you overheard
what it was that they've just been talking about."

"Oh, yes," said the waiter. "One of them said—"

"Hold on," broke in the American. "I don't want you to
tell me yet. I want to see if my deductions are correct.
Now here's the way I've figured out their conversation:
One of them—the one with the beard and the educated
eyebrows—is an inventor. I'm sure he's an inventor. And
lately he perfected a new aeroplane—an improvement on
all the older models. He described its design at some
length. From his gestures I could make out that the pro-
peller revolved much more rapidly than most propellers
can revolve. The trial trip must have taken place very

recently. Everything went well until the machine had ascended to a great height. Then something broke.

"Down, down, down came the ill-fated aircraft. It struck the earth with a tremendous crash. It was dashed to pieces. The aëronaut—evidently a friend of the inventor—was instantly killed. His body was horribly mangled. It was a terrible spectacle, a terrible tragedy. The poor man is still filled with distress and dismay; probably his nervous system will never be the same again. And never again will he have anything to do with aircraft—he is through forever. His table-mate, listening to the recital, has been almost overcome by emotion. He, too, is grief-stricken. Now then, tell me whether I'm right?"

"Not exactly," stated the waiter. "What happened between them was this: The tall gentleman has been explaining to his companion that for luncheon today he had two soft-boiled eggs—and one of them was bad!"

Mark Twain
Italian Without a Master 1904

IT IS ALMOST A FORTNIGHT now that I am domiciled in a mediæval villa in the country, a mile or two from Florence. I cannot speak the language; I am too old now to learn how, also too busy when I am busy, and too indolent when I am not; wherefore some will imagine that I am having a dull time of it. But it is not so. The "help" are all natives; they talk Italian to me, I answer in English; I do not understand them, they do not understand me, consequently no harm is done, and everybody is satisfied. In order to be just and fair, I throw in an Italian word when I have one, and this has a good influence. I get the word out of the morning paper. I have to use it while it is fresh, for I find that Italian words do not keep in this climate. They fade towards night, and next morning they are gone. But it is no matter; I get a new one out of thé paper before breakfast, and thrill the domestics with it while it lasts. I have no dictionary, and I do not want one; I can select my words by the sound, or by orthographic aspect. Many of them have a French or German or English look, and these are the ones I enslave for the day's service. That is, as a rule. Not always. If I find a learnable phrase that has an imposing look and warbles musically along I do not care to know the meaning of it; I pay it out to the first applicant, knowing that if I pronounce it carefully he will understand it, and that's enough.

Yesterday's word was *avanti.* It sounds Shakespearian, and probably means Avaunt and quit my sight. To-day I have a whole phrase: *sono dispiacentissimo.* I do not know what it means, but it seems to fit in everywhere and give satisfaction. Although as a rule my words and phrases are good for one day and train only, I have several that stay by me all the time, for some unknown reason, and these come very handy when I get into a long conversation and need things to fire up with in monotonous stretches. One of the best ones is *Dov' è il gatto.* It nearly always produces a pleasant surprise, therefore I save it up for places where I want to express applause or admiration. The fourth word has a French sound, and I think the phrase means "that takes the cake."

Karel Capek
In the Hand of Fate 1929

THE SAYING GOES: if you travel anywhere learn the local language so as better to penetrate the soul of the people, and things of that sort. Well, you can just as easily penetrate people's souls if you travel to the next town. There you'll understand all the stupidities folks utter and you can ask them all sorts of superfluous questions, e.g., what is the name of that mountain, or how many minutes late is the train?

I travel through the land of Italy unburdened by such interests: my capacity and time suffice only to learn Italian numerals (of course only the lowest), and even this acquisition vexes me at times since it disturbs my peaceful resignation to the will of fate. In international hotels you can always make yourself understood in French. But there are places more interesting than all the hotels in the world, and there you can't inquire or make yourself understood or ask anyone for anything; there you rely upon people to provide you with food, drink, and lodgings and to take you somewhere—how and where, that is of course up to them, not you. You entrust yourself to them as a dumb, helpless creature incapable of choice, self-defense, or insult. In return they give you food and drink, protection and lodging. You accept everything with a thousand-fold more gratitude than if you'd ordered it in a lordly manner.

You travel with the simplicity of St. Francis. Because you cannot speak you cannot desire anything from people. To desire next-to-nothing is true humility and resignation; to demand no more than a mouthful and lodgings, to accept everything they provide, and to trust that everyone means well by you—that means freedom from anxiety and leads to a whole series of virtues. You are modest and thankful, unassuming and quiet, satisfied and confident; gone is all your arrogance, elation, and impatience, all your complicated and selfish fastidiousness; you are in the power of others and, consequently, in the hand of fate. You cannot ask whether this railway carriage goes only to Caldare or Xirbi or Bicocca, because you do not know how to express it. So you sit and trust that "they" know better than you and will take you to charming and important places. You do not choose food or lodgings: you accept what others give you and, presto, they give you the best they can. You want to pay and they name an incomprehensible sum: you do not know if they said 1 lira 50 or 50 lire, so you give them all your money and they take what they know is proper. They are very trustworthy: they take out only 1.50. No one cheated me, except for a cab-driver in Posilippo. Immediately, seeing that I myself simply had no power of abuse, the whole town collected around this rascal and upbraided him.

There are indeed complicated situations, e.g., one may want to know if there's a steamer leaving Salerno today. On my inquiry, the waiter at the café did not know the particulars, so he called to some people in the street, who came and sat round me, ordered *café noir*, and deliberated as to what I wanted. I said I wanted to go to Naples; they nodded and consulted and then accompanied me in a body to the train, where I had to distribute visiting cards by way of souvenirs. Sometimes they looked after me, as if I were a small boy, like that old lady at Siena who spoke to me in baby language, with infinitives and vigorous gestures. My relations with them were extraordinarily good: I never disputed with them nor they with me.

Believe me in this: with a little simplicity and patience one may travel anywhere in the world. On the whole— with exceptions—it is possible to trust people: nothing strengthens optimism more than this experience. It would have been delightful to have known Italian, but of course I would have seen less, because I would have wandered about less and not lingered in regions of which Baedeker says nothing. One takes a tram in the wrong direction and instead of arriving at some dull park with a magnificent view he finds himself in the commercial quarter and lands in some unutterable mass of dirt, such as Arenella, more astonished than if he'd contemplated the subtropical vegetation of Palermo Gardens. Yes, to roam about and be dumb and helpless in the hand of fate is a great delight and a great advantage.

Irene Kampen
Write This Down 1965

G OT A PENCIL?" the manager of the Piggly-Wiggly meat department said to me. "Okay—write this down. Ferragambino's."

I opened my notebook and under "Italy" I wrote down *Ferragambino's. (Manager of Piggly-Wiggly Meat Department).*

"It's a little restaurant in Settignano," the manager said. "they serve the best fettucini in the world. This place is off the beaten track, not all crapped up with American tourists."

"We aren't going to Settignano," I said.

He stared at me.

"You aren't going to Settignano?" he said. "What's the point of going to Italy if you miss Settignano?"

"Cook's didn't put it on the itinerary," I said.

"Itinerary!" he said. "I bet they've got you booked into every tourist trap in Italy, up to and including Venice."

"Venice is no good?" I said.

"Venice!" he said scornfully. "Do you know what Venice is?"

"No," I said. "What is Venice?"

"Venice is Coney Island," the manager of the Piggly-Wiggly meat department said, "with pigeons."

Ludwig Bemelmans

THE THREE BIG ONES

ᵃ⋅Rome

᛬Most European countries have one capital toward which the rest of the country leans, sometimes so perilously the provincials have to hold on for dear life. London, Paris, Lisbon, Prague. But that's not good enough for the Italians. The nation of once great city-states couldn't settle for just one all-encompassing metropolis. They had to have one capital for ruins and religion, another for art, and yet another for romanticism. And that's just their tourist capitals. They also have their capital of fashion and industry, their capital of automobiles, their capital of crime, and to top it all off they put the symbol of their otherwise not so leaning country in yet another capital, whose name sounds awfully much like what we think of as their national dish. And you wonder why they talk so fast! The Briton and the Frenchman can slowly, lovingly say the two syllables that constitute his capital; the Italian has to rush his way through Roma, Firenza, Venezia, Milano, Torino, Palermo, and Pisa, twenty syllables in all.

   Now take a breath while I introduce our section on Rome. Better yet, help me decide where to start. Chronologically? with the classical ruins, the Colosseum, the Forum, the Pantheon, all those places where so much happened so long ago as well as in all those films of our youth? Geographically? going from hill to hill, up and down all those steps, Spanish and otherwise, through all those piazzas and past all those fountains? Religiously? starting in the land that isn't Rome, that isn't even Italy, but that's probably more widely known: the Vatican? No, the best place to start is where each of us starts, especial-

ly when we first arrive somewhere that we're sure we'll know when we see it, we've seen its likeness on so many restaurant walls: our expectations. And whose expectations are greater than Charles Dickens'?

Charles Dickens
There It Lay 1844

A SHORT RIDE brought us to Ronciglione, a little town like a large pig-sty, where we passed the night. Next morning at seven o'clock, we started for Rome.

As soon as we were out of the pig-sty, we entered on the Campagna Romana, an undulating flat (as you know), where few people can live; and where, for miles and miles, there is nothing to relieve the terrible monotony and gloom. Of all kinds of country that could, by possibility, lie outside the gates of Rome, this is the aptest and fittest burial-ground for the Dead City. So sad, so quiet, so sullen; so secret in its covering up of great masses of ruin, and hiding them; so like the waste places into which the men possessed with devils used to go to howl and rend themselves in the old days of Jerusalem. We had to traverse thirty miles of this Campagna; and for two-and-twenty we went on and on, seeing nothing but now and then a lonely house, or a villainous-looking shepherd with matted hair all over his face, and himself wrapped to the chin in a frowzy brown mantle, tending his sheep. At the end of that distance, we stopped to refresh the horses and to get some lunch in a common malaria-shaken, despondent little public-house, whose every inch of wall and beam, inside, was (according to custom) painted and decorated in a way so miserable that every room looked like the wrong side of another room, and, with its wretched imitation of drapery and lop-sided little daubs of lyres, seemed to have been plundered from behind the scenes of some travelling circus.

When we were fairly off again, we began, in a perfect fever, to strain our eyes for Rome; and when, after another mile or two, the Eternal City appeared, at length, in the distance, it looked like—I am half afraid to write the word—like LONDON!!! There it lay, under a thick cloud, with innumerable towers, and steeples, and roofs of houses, rising up into the sky, and high above them all, one Dome. I swear, that keenly as I felt the seeming absurdity of the comparison, it was so like London, at that distance, that if you could have shown it me in a glass I should have taken it for nothing else.

Once you've gotten over the fact that you're actually in Rome, you'll want to come down to earth (or climb a hill, as the case may be) and check into your hotel. Here's the incomparable Art Buchwald to tell you what to expect.

Art Buchwald
How to Be Obnoxious But Happy 1959

IT HAS ALWAYS BEEN MY POLICY to urge restraint on the part of the tourist when traveling on the Continent. As people who suffer both from superiority and inferiority complexes (consult your local psychiatrist for which one), we are very conscious of what other Europeans think of us, and the majority of us try to cause as little trouble as possible so we won't give our country a bad name.

But now I must reverse myself and give instructions on how to be obnoxious and happy while traveling. To begin with, Europe goes every year into what is commonly called "the height of the tourist season." Hotel managers and reception clerks who a few months before were wailing about the lack of tourist business are now swamped with requests for rooms which they cannot possibly fill, and so we find the confirmed reservation slip is in many cases not worth the paper it is printed on.

As my good friend Al Capp told me a few years ago, the best thing to do with a confirmed reservation slip when you have no room is to spread it out on the sidewalk in front of the hotel and go to sleep on it. You'll either embarrass the hotel into giving you a room or you'll be hauled off to the local jug, where at least you'll have a roof over your head.

Sometimes there are so many people with confirmed reservation slips on the sidewalk that you may have to sleep in front of another hotel. But you have no legal right if you do this, because the sidewalk space in front of each hotel is reserved only for people who have confirmed reservations for that hotel.

Rome is probably one of the most difficult cities in Europe in which to find a hotel room. Despite the fact that tourist business has quadrupled in the past seven years and airlines have put on extra planes to handle the people, no one has thought to build a new hotel. This leads people with confirmed reservations to sleep on every available piece of sidewalk in town, and makes strolling during the late evening and early hours of the morning very difficult.

Then what is a tourist to do when he arrives in the city and discovers that the room he has booked three months ago does not exist?

Being nice about it won't even get you a place on the sidewalk. The only thing to do is be obnoxious. The more obnoxious you are, the better chance you have of sleeping in a bed that night. Not only should you be obnoxious about it, but you should be loud and obnoxious.

The best method of getting a hotel room in Rome with a confirmed reservation is to scream at the top of your lungs so that everyone in the lobby will hear you. The louder you scream the more obnoxious you become and the more nervous the receptionist clerk will be. Pretty soon the manager, who has been down in the cellar supervising the printing of confirmed reservation slips, will rush upstairs and you will be given the room you were promised, or a better one.

The thing to remember is—EVERY HOTEL HAS AN EMPTY ROOM AND THE PERSON WHO SCREAMS THE LOUDEST IN THE LOBBY IS THE PERSON WHO GETS IT.

Some tourists become embarrassed when they see a fellow countryman making a scene in the lobby of a hotel, but they are usually people who have their hotel room and can be noble about the whole thing. When a tourist is seen shouting in the lobby of a hotel, he is more to be pitied than censured. He is only trying to stay off the sidewalk.

Many people were shocked at the way I behaved in the lobby of a Roman hotel one Sunday afternoon, not long ago, but they will be glad to know that all the screaming was not in vain.

Although I woke up three concierges as well as twelve tourists who were trying to sleep in the lobby because they had no rooms, I am happy to report that after only four minutes of yelling and waving my arms I was ushered up to a lovely room with bath and was treated as an honored guest after that.

They even cashed a personal check for fifty dollars for me, which shows what they thought of me.

OK, you're settled now and raring to go. It's all out there waiting for you. No, not the purse-snatchers; the sights! The churches, the ruins, the stores. To be sure you take the tour appropriate to your interests and desires we have lined up classic American humorists Irvin S. Cobb, who took his sharp tongue to Europe not long before the First World War broke out, and Will Rogers, who knew

Irvin S. Cobb
Trying to Imagine 1913

THE GUIDEBOOKS SAY that no visitor to Rome should miss seeing the Golden House of Nero. When a guidebook tries to be humorous it only succeeds in being foolish. Practical jokes are out of place in a guidebook anyway. Imagine a large, old-fashioned brick smokehouse, which has been struck by lightning, burned to the roots and buried in the wreckage, and the site used as a pasture land for goats for a great many years; imagine the debris as having been dug out subsequently until a few of the foundation lines are visible; surround the whole with distressingly homely buildings of a modern aspect, and stir in a miscellaneous seasoning of beggars and loafers and souvenir venders—and you have the Golden House where Nero meant to round out a life already replete with incident and abounding in romance, but was deterred from so doing by reason of being cut down in the midst of his activities at a comparatively early age.

In the presence of the Golden House of Nero I did my level best to recreate before my mind's eye the scenes that had been enacted here once on a time. I tried to picture this moldy, knee-high wall as a great glittering palace; and yonder broken roadbed as a splendid Roman highway; and those American-looking tenements on the surrounding hills as the marble dwellings of the emperors; and all the broken pillars and shattered porticoes in the distance as arches of triumph and temples of the gods. I tried to convert the clustering mendicants into barbarian prisoners clanking by, chained at wrist and neck and ankle; I sought to imagine the pestersome

28

flower venders as being vestal virgins; the two unkempt policemen who loafed nearby, as centurions of the guard; the passing populace as grave senators in snowy togas; the flaunting underwear on the many clotheslines as silken banners and gilded trappings. I could not make it. I tried until I was lame in both legs and my back was strained. It was no go.

If I had been a poet or a historian, or a person full of Chianti, I presume I might have done it; but I am no poet and I had not been drinking. All I could think of was that the guide on my left had eaten too much garlic and that the guide on my right had not eaten enough. So in self-defense I went away and ate a few strands of garlic myself; for I had learned the great lesson of the proverb:

When in Rome be an aroma!

Will Rogers
No Disrespect Intended 1926

MY DEAR MR. PRESIDENT: Calvin, I wish you could see Rome. It's the oldest uncivilized Town in the world. New York is just as uncivilized, but it's not as old as Rome. Rome has been held by every Nation in the World at one time or another for no reason at all. Between you and I, I think some of them give it up without much of a struggle.

Rome has more Churches and less preaching in them than any City in the World. Everybody wants to see where Saint Peter was buried, but nobody wants to try to live like him.

There is 493 Guidebooks sold to every Testament. They would rather take Baedeker's word than Moses'.

The headliners in Roman History is Julius Caesar, Mark Antony and Nero. Then Mussolini come along and made Bush Leaguers out of all of them.

Rome was built on seven hills. Every prominent Roman had a little hill all his own. History records, and local gossip has added to history, that coming home after a hard and exciting night at the baths, there has been Romans that dident find the right hill. That's what made Roman history interesting. There is only six of these hills left today. Some Roman went out of the back window so fast one night that he took the hill with him. That's the inside story. But of course present History says that the Barbarians took not only all the assembled Romans but the hill as well with them.

I tried to find out who the Barbarians were. From the best that I could learn, Barbarians were a race of people that stole from you. If you stole from the barbarians, you were indexed in your History as a Christian. * * *

In other words, Rome is really not what it's cracked up to be. History was no more right in reporting the happenings of Rome than it has been in some of the Cities we have heard of. Now everybody goes to Rome on account of its old historical record. Now you know and I know it ain't history that you are out to study. You are out to make History. What you want to plan is, some day some Guy will be studying you instead of you studying him. Any Yap can read what somebody else has done; but can he get out and do something himself, that anybody would read about, even if they dident have anything else to read? * * *

They got a lot of things they call Forums. They are where the Senators used to meet and debate—on disarmament, I suppose. They say there was some bloody mob scenes and fights in there. Well, that's one thing they got us licked on. Calling each other a liar and heaving an inkstand is about the extent of our Senatorial gladiators' warlike accomplishments.

I dident know before I got there, and they told me all this—that Rome had Senators. Now I know why it declined. There is quite an argument there over the exact spot of Caesar's Death. Some say that Caesar was not slain in the Senate; they seem to think that he had gone over to a Senatorial Investigation meeting at some Committee room, and that that is where Brutus gigged him. The moral of the whole thing seems to be to stay away from investigations.

I also picked up a little scandal there that I know you won't turn a deaf ear to. About this particular case, they are saying around Rome now, but they hope it don't get back to any of his people, that Brutus was Caesar's natural son, and that Cassius was a sort of a brother-in-law without Portfolio. Then they showed where Mark Antony delivered his oration, which, as it wasent written till 500 years after he was supposed to say it, there was some chance there of misinterpretation. I have heard some of our Public men's speeches garbled in next morning's paper.

Then they speak of a Cicero. I don't know exactly what he did. His name sounds kinder like he was window dresser. Then there was the intellectual tracks of Vergil. I guess you had a crack at him while you was up at Amherst. Vergil must have been quite a fellow, but he dident know enough to put his stuff in English like Shakespeare did, so you don't hear much of him any more, only in high school and roasting-ear Colleges, where he is studied more and remembered less than any single person. I bet you yourself right now, Mr. President, don't know over three of Vergil's words. E Pluribus Unum will just about let you out. I never even got to him in school, and I remember that much. Ask Vare when he gets in there to quote you some of Vergil.

There is quite a few of those old Forums besides the Senate one. Evidently they were afflicted with a House of Representatives, a Supreme Court and a Foreign Relations Committee. 'Course it's just a lot of old brokendown Marble now. Most of the old pieces are big enough so the Tourists can't carry them away; that's the only reason they are there. A lot of them are being torn down to put in modern plumbing. * * *

These Romans loved blood. What money is to an American, blood was to a Roman. A Roman was never so happy as when he saw somebody bleeding. That was his sense of humor, just like ours is. If we see a fellow slip and fall and maby break his leg, why, that's a yell to us; or his hat blow off and he can't get it. Well, that's the way the Romans were. Where we like to see you lose your hat, they loved to see you leave a right arm and a left leg in the possession of a Tiger and then try to make the fence unaided.

The Emperor set in his box, and a lot of Ladies set in another great big Box, and during the festivities they would announce with their thumbs whether the man was to go on to his death or let him live. The women had the first guess, but the Emperor he had the veto power; he passed on the things as final. You see, they used their thumbs for something besides buttoning up their clothes. If they held their thumbs down, you passed out Poco Pronto; but if they held them up, why, you left your phone and address where you could be reached the following Sunday afternoon. There was no Dempsey stuff of four years between combats, no dickering over terms. The gate receipts went to the Emperor and you went to the cemetery.

'Course this old Colosseum is a great old building. They have stole enough off of it to build everything else in Rome. Poor Mussolini come in so late in history that there wasent anything left for him at all. Everything in Rome was stolen from somebody at some time. It's just a question of who's got it last. * * *

Now there is a forum there called Stargens, or something like that, and it's down in the ground with a high wall around it, and a lot of old Marble columns broken off and standing and laying around. Well, they have a habit of taking all the old stray cats and the neighbors feed them. It has now become known as the Forum of the Cats. Now to me that was a real place. Here was something alive. I used to walk down there to see what the old kitties were doing, and at night I went two or three times. You could see an old tomcat setting up on top of a Roman column where maby Mark Antony had delivered one of his monologues. This old Tabby would be squatting up there, howling for no reason at all, just like a typical politician, and just as much sense to it too. Now that was great to me to see those Cats. I don't want to convey any disrespect to those who have passed beyond, but I would rather see one live Cat than a dozen dead Romans. * * *

Yours devotedly,

WILL

Even for the classicist and the shopper, there's nothing in Rome like St. Peter's. The largest church in the world, the center of one of the largest and most widespread religions, the only place any of us could imagine ever having an audience with anyone. And then there's its unforgettable Sistine Chapel. Alexander Woollcott— humorist, critic, and leader of the old Round Table at New York's Algonquin Hotel—has a humorous story to tell about his visit to St. Peter's with F. P. A., alias Franklin P. Adams, the father in many ways of the great American humorists of the 20s and 30s. But first, novelist, historian, and artist Stephen Longstreet provides an unusual perspective on the world's most famous chapel: an eavesdropping look at the way a couple of Germans approached great art early in World War Two.

Stephen Longstreet
An Insatiable Appetite for Details 1941

A GREAT MANY PEOPLE COME to look at the Sistine Chapel. Germans with their damn cameras and Italians crossing themselves at the symbols (for they can't very well understand the art, being mostly women in black—tired, childbearing women come to have a few private words with Him). Americans stand impressed, Englishmen nod to one another. Only the Germans talk art jargon.

My German is torn lace with gaps in it to throw volumes of Schiller through. But I stood near two large crop-haired blond tourists who were tracing every crack with the aid of a guide book. They had an insatiable appetite for detail. Detached granules of color floated high over us.

"Wonderful *(wunderbar)*," said one.

"Beg pardon *(bitte?)?*" answered the other.

"Wonderful."

"Organized space. Very well done."

"Solid color."

"Ceiling looks none too strong."

"It's lasted a long time. But I suppose one good air bomb and..."

"Nonsense. These old buildings are solid stone twelve feet thick. An air bomb—say, five hundred pounds—would only shake the building."

"Not if dropped with a delayed fuse so that it could enter and then explode."

"Ah..."

"Ja. Behüt euch Gott."

They looked up at Jehovah with his Jewish curls, breathing life into the non-Aryan body of Adam. They closed their cameras and, arm in arm, the art lovers went away, patrician and scholar, both very sure of themselves.

Alexander Woollcott
As Easy As Rolling Off
a Travelogue 1928

BACK IN NEW YORK after many mid-summer weeks spent idly roaming the pleasant palaces of France and Italy, back after a revel of turquoise lakes, crêpes suzettes, nightingales, hat pools, green lizards, rates of exchange, aperitifs, Raquel Meller, et al, I sit down at home each Fall amid my memories and face with dismay the fact that I cannot write a travel article. I am not an Isaac F. Marcosson. I am not even a Clayton Hamilton. I simply cannot do it.

If, on the day in 1925 when I wandered into Rome, I had been a Marcosson, I would have telephoned Mussolini and said: "Mussolini, what are you doing for lunch?" And, what with a few general generalisms about the Fascisti and a note or two hurriedly scribbled on the back of a menu card, the thing would have been done.

Instead, I knew that F. P. A. was in Rome. So I telephoned him. Wherefore, the lunch was both tasty and hilarious. But there was no copy in it.

I might have come back in the grand manner of Professor Hamilton to disconcert the miserable stay-at-homes by asking loftily: "Have you ever stood bareheaded in the nave at Amiens? Have you ever climbed the Acropolis by moonlight? Have you ever walked with whispers into the hushed presence of the Ferrara Madonna of Bellini?" I am not sure but I believe that at this point the stay-at-homes are supposed to say: "No," and burst into tears of chagrin and humiliation. I fancy that I, too, might attempt this crushing technique, for in my feebler moments I have done quite a bit of sightseeing. But, unfortunately, it is always the undistinguished venture of some unpre-meditated day in a spot unmarked in any guidebook which haunts me longest in the afteryears. And even when I do set my reluctant feet in some beaten path, something invariably goes wrong. I have great sympathy for my good neighbor Percy Hammond, who did his best one summer to follow the Clayton Hamilton standard by trudging bareheaded to the Colosseum in the moonlight. But even as he stood where Caesar stood, while his thoughts mutely summoned all the ghosts of the grandeur that was Rome, the voice that broke the stillness was no voice of the past but the shrill and anxious clamor of a fellow tourist crying out of the shadowy corridor: *"Wo ist Heine? Wo ist Heine?"*

I think I will remember longest the casual, unhistoric day spent in a villa perched on the hills in Chianti, half way between Florence and Siena, the bustling, pleasant country home of the Marquesa Viviana della Robbia, where the tenant farmers till the sloping fields and tread the incomparable grapes much as they have done since the Etruscan days when Rome was not. The cool casks of Chianti, each taller than a man, standing in rows in the chill caves beneath the house, the olive trees drooping sleepily in the afternoon sun, the old tortoise who, the gardener swears, once looked upon Napoleon as he rode by—these blur and blend into the background for the fair daughter of the house whose face is a composite of the portraits of all the lovely ladies in the Uffizi Gallery.

And taught in her childhood by an American gover-ness, it was a startling thing to find that to this Italian girl, America was as romantic and haze-hung a vista as Italy might be for you or for me, that the tales of it were as glamorous to her as all the legends of Italy could be to us, and that to her ears, to quote a fondly remembered book, there was all the music and the mystery in such a word as Indiana, say, as we hear in the name of Vallombrosa. She subscribed faithfully to the *Ladies' Home Journal*, bought all the records of Irving Berlin's tunes and would not let us go till we had taught her how to shoot craps and had explained why, when it became vitally important for us to throw a four, we knelt and called aloud upon a strange patron saint whom we addressed familiarly as "*piccolo Giusseppe.*"

I would not give up the pleasant memory of such a day for all the Madonnas in Florence, for all the naves from Amiens to Milan. And even when, mindful of my trade and the need of enlarging experiences, I do deliberately seek a great occasion, something always goes wrong. Consider how unutterably wrong things went that summer when I journeyed to Rome to attend the beatification services in St. Peter's.

That mishap befell on the afternoon in June when all Christendom seemed come to Rome for the beatification of Bernadette, the little peasant *religieuse* who years ago came wide-eyed from the woods at Lourdes to tell the tale of a vision which has since made that spot a shrine for the halt and the blind from the four corners of the earth. Now on the long road to sainthood, Bernadette has reached the stage of beatification. Wherefore, beneath the relentless sun the faithful and unnumbered thousands waited at the door for admission to St. Peter's.

Proud neighbors of Bernadette from the Pyrénée foothills, priests from Martinique and Indo-China, grand Spanish matrons in mantillas and pious pilgrims from Quebec—these milled in the shadeless square. And deep embedded in the mass were three would-be onlookers from New York—F. P. A., Mrs. F. P. A. and your humble servant. We had been wedged in that slow moving multitude for more than an hour and were wondering cynically how pleasant the swimming was at Great Neck that afternoon when we chanced to examine our damp firm-clutched cards of admission and read with sinking hearts that only those might enter the great portals who were appropriately clad in black. This was dire news for the three frolicsome young things in fairly white tennis flannels.

But returning were as tedious as go o'er. It would take less time, ruffle fewer tempers and break fewer ribs to go on to the door and be thrown out than to turn and try to fight our way back through the crowd which now stretched as far as the eye could see. Yet, when at last the tide of the crowd did deposit us on the threshold of St. Peter's, we might have been clad in gaudy bathing suits and still have been swept helpless past the oblivious guards into the great, cool, waiting basilica.

It was all astir with a festivity of preparation, incomparably gay with immense banners of scarlet flung from the highest points of the pillars to the floor. There was the hubbub of scurrying thousands as the spectators were shown to their seats, ours being on long wooden benches placed for the occasion in the transept. They were of such height that, by standing upon them, we could see the long aisle where soon that great procession would file by on its way to the altar. So many stood up in this wise that soon there was just such a hum of "Down in front. Down in front," as you might hear at any Army-Navy game. Unfortunately the Italians in their foolish way say *Giu* when they mean down, and as they pronounce this in their own odd fashion, it was a chorus of "Jew, Jew, Jew" that we heard on all sides of us. This embarrassed F. P. A. considerably. He could vent his feelings only by muttering under his breath, "So's your old man."

Then, with the Swiss guards in all their upholstery clearing the transept aisle of the final stragglers, and with the royal troops forming the wall of the lane along which the procession was to come, the trumpets sounded and the great spectacle began. With thunderous peals from the organ, with shrill, sweet piping from choirs invisible, with Cardinals flowing like water, the Pope came down the aisle, borne aloft in triumph, and was greeted, to my intense and delighted surprise, not by prostrate and silent adoration, but by just such a gust of hearty, friendly applause and cheering as might greet a halfback borne in triumph off the field.

It was when this climax in the procession had swept on out of sight that we began to wonder apprehensively how we were ever to join the car that was trustingly waiting outside to carry us to tea under the umbrella pines of the Villa Doria. If we could not slip away then and there, if once we were caught again in that vicious throng, there would be no hope for us. Was there, haply, some accessible and unobtrusive sidedoor through which we could vanish into the open air? We held parley on the subject with the nearest Swiss guard. How could it be managed? He looked at us with the tired surprise usually reserved for the questioning by the village idiot. You just walk out, the Swiss guard patiently explained. Down the main aisle? Down the main aisle, of course.

We were all abashed by the prospect of so conspicuous an exit. The choirs flooded the nave with a fresh cascade of song. We wavered. The guard grew suddenly animated. "Come, come," he muttered. "You have no time to waste." And he pushed us on our way. Thus, unwilling and really bewildered, we debouched into the main aisle.

And at that final moment, as though the whole ceremony had been timed just for our arrival in the aisle, something happened. I do not know what it was. Perhaps the Pope had turned and faced the multitude. Perhaps the signal was given for the procession to return. At all events, we had no sooner stepped into the aisle than the soldiers closed ranks, brought up their swords to attention, and we were trapped in a corridor of bristling steel.

Behind us, bearing down on us, was the clustered dignity of Holy Church. Ahead—a lane of pointing swords and an infinitude of glistening porphyry— stretched the road to Rome, the only road to Rome. It is I suppose, the longest aisle in the world. I do not know how long but it is my present impression that its length is about the distance from Grant's Tomb to the State Capitol in Albany. And we had to walk it. With feet grown suddenly leaden, with knees that had become oddly unhinged, we had to walk that aisle alone. And just as we had begun to believe that after all, locomotion was not a lost art, something else, something worse happened. I suppose the Pope had started up the aisle after us. I know only that at some signal the soldiers as one man dropped each on his knee and thrust his sword into the air in salute, thrust his sword into the air at us. After that, everything is a blank. The next thing I remember is that we were bowling along the road toward the Villa Doria. But I could not help noticing that the raven hair of F. P. A. had turned snow-white since noon.

A Wager

No ride on the Appian Way is regarded as complete without half an hour's stop at the Catacombs of Saint Calixtus; so we stopped. Guided by a brown Trappist, and all of us bearing twisted tapers in our hands, we descended by stone steps deep under the skin of the earth and wandered through dim, dank underground passages, where thousands of early Christians had lived and hid, and held clandestine worship before rude stone altars, and had died and been buried—died in a highly unpleasant fashion, some of them.

The experience was impressive, but malarial. Coming away from there I had an argument with a fellow American. He said that if we had these Catacombs in America we should undoubtedly enlarge them and put in band stands and lunch places, and altogether make them more attractive for picnic parties and Sunday excursionists. I contended, on the other hand, that if they were in America the authorities would close them up and protect the moldered bones of those early Cristians from the vulgar gaze and prying fingers of every impious relic hunter who might come along. The dispute rose higher and grew warmer until I offered to bet him fifty dollars that I was right and he was wrong. He took me up promptly—he had sporting instincts; I'll say that for him—and we shook hands on it then and there to bind the wager. I expect to win that bet. —*Irvin S. Cobb, 1913*

Rube Goldberg

❧Venice

(The following selection accompanies the illustration on the opposite page.)

Rube Goldberg and Sam Boal
Romantic Venice 1954

THERE IS LITTLE DOUBT THAT VENICE is the most romantic city in Europe. Flung like a necklace of pearls across the Venetian lagoon, the city of islands is all things to all men. Some poets have turned to fire at the thought of Venice; others have turned to ice. (This may account for the high mortality rate on poets in Venice.) Four centuries of painters, their eyes fevered with the colors of Venice, have tried to capture it on canvas. The music of Venice—the soft lapping of the ripples in the canals, the gentle cries of the birds sweeping through the skies, and the tinkle of ice in Harry's Bar—mingle with the murmur of lovers' sighs in the fragrant air over Venice.

Take your loved one through Venice in a *gondola* (Italian word for gondola) while the boatman chants his age-old song of romance and the palaces of the ancient doges drift by. Discover how well Venice deserves its title—The Biggest Tunnel of Love in the World.

❧*Romance is to the humorist as blood is to the vampire. The only difference is that the humorist is a little more fun to be with and he doesn't go for the jugular quite as often.*

Paris is full of romance, but it's also full of crazy drivers and politics and modern art, whose only romantic attribute is its price. There are no drivers in Venice, and its politics and art are hardly modern. It's a world of doges and cardinals and an empire that seems more unreal than Rome's, based as it was on ships rather than troops. It is a city of water, of canals and lagoons, a city that other cities say they're like: Bruges, the Venice of the north; Bangkok, the Venice of the east; Venice, the Venice of California. But more even than water, Venice, the city of Venus, is the city of love. And humorists prey on love like vampires prey on... no, I've already used that one.

The city's reigning princes of love are the gondoliers. They may look like they belong in Disneyland, but they act more like cabbies in New York City. Irene Kampen's introduction to Venice was via water cabbie.

Irene Kampen
Welcome to Venezia 1965

THE WAGON-LITS COOK'S REPRESENTATIVE had patent-leather hair and smelled deliciously of gardenias. He maneuvered us through the throng of passengers and porters out to the wide marble steps of the station, all the while murmuring *"Bella! Bellissima!"* and casting expressive glances up at Chris.

I sensed that a pinch was imminent.

Once outside, he produced a policeman's whistle from a pocket of his uniform and gave a shrill blast on it. The crowd of waiting gondoliers began to row furiously towards us, smashing into each other's gondolas, making threatening gestures at one another with the gondola oars, and shouting Italian curses back and forth across the water.

The Cook's representative took a pink handkerchief out of another pocket and mopped his perspiring forehead. He then carefully refolded the handkerchief, put it back in his pocket, and said a long sentence to Chris in Italian.

"*Ciao,*" Chris said back. It was something she'd picked up from an old Audrey Hepburn movie about Rome.

"What did he say to you?" I asked.

"I think it was something about sex," Chris said.

"I'd love to find out what perfume he's wearing," I said. "It's heavenly."

"*Parla Italiano?*" the Cook's representative asked me.

I shrugged eloquently, to convey that I had studied the language twenty years ago in Abraham Lincoln High School, Brooklyn, New York, but had forgotten it.

"Your sister, she is very high," the Cook's man said.

"She's not my sister," I said. "She's my daughter."

"Dau-tair?" he repeated. "Please, what is this dau-tair?"

"Me mother," I said, pointing to myself. I pointed to Chris. "She daughter."

"Me Tarzan," Chris said, "you Jane."

The Cook's man reeled back dramatically and flung his arms wide in amazement.

"Impossible!" he said. "You are too young and beautiful yourself to have such a massive daughter!"

I noticed that one of the gondoliers had jumped onto the prow of another gondola that had collided with his and was trying to choke the other gondolier to death. Nobody seemed to be paying any attention to them.

"A beautiful girl," the Cook's representative whispered to me, giving a wink in Chris's direction. "A virgin, one presupposes?"

"*Che sera, sera,*" I said.

The winning gondolier had now leaped back to his own boat and rowed over to the steps where we were waiting. I looked down and saw that his gondola was tastefully furnished with a wicker loveseat and a black leather office chair with ball-and-claw feet. A vase of plastic tulips was fastened to the prow with Scotch tape.

The Cook's representative tossed our valises into the gondola, handed us in after the luggage, and stood on the steps crying *"Arrivederci!"* and blowing kisses after us as we sailed off.

Our gondolier, who was bald and fat and wore a dirty blue-and-white striped T-shirt, threaded his way through the mass of gondolas clustered around the station, shouting Italian obscenities at his fellow-gondoliers and shaking his fist threateningly whenever another boat blocked our way. We turned into a side canal and narrowly missed colliding with a hugh gondola loaded to the gunwales with cases of Pepsi-Cola.

"Che Diavolo!" our gondolier shouted. *"Biscoro! Porco mondo!"*

The Pepsi-Cola gondolier spit expressively into the water. At that moment another gondola carrying half a dozen female tourists sailed by, and a lady in the prow whipped out her motion-picture camera and began shooting footage of the argument. As our two boats came abreast Chris and I obligingly waved into the lens, and the lady waved back and called over to ask where we were from. We told her we were from Connecticut. She said she and her friends were from Columbus, Ohio, and we all exchanged farewell waves as our gondolier steered around the corner into the Grand Canal, swerving adroitly to avoid a large garbage gondola that was bearing down on us.

"The Grand Canal!" I said to Chris. "Look—there's the Bridge of Sighs!"

"Not the Bridge of Sighs, Signora," the gondolier said, leaning over and breathing garlic at us. "Bridge of Sighs is more further. This is Rialto Bridge."

"I wonder how come they call the Bridge of Sighs the Bridge of Sighs," Chris said.

"I think it has something to do with Dante sighing at Beatrice when he passed her on it," I said.

The gondolier frowned at me.

"Is called Bridge of Sighs because prisoners going to dungeons would walk across for last time," he said. "They would look out at beautiful city of Venezia and give a big sigh. Like so."

He put his hand over his heart and gave a big sigh, releasing another gust of garlic.

"And there's the famous Ponte Vecchio!" I said, pointing to a bridge ahead of us.

"Ponte Vecchio is in Firenze," the gondolier told me firmly. "We are now in Venezia. *Prego*."

He went back to his rowing.

"I want to buy some Italian sandals," Chris said, "and a pair of blue sunglasses and a white linen skirt and a yellow raffia sweater."

"I want to buy a gondolier's hat," I said.

"And a present for Moose," Chris said.

A man in a passing gondola stood up, aimed a camera at us, and snapped our picture. He winked at me and tossed a folded piece of paper across the water into my lap.

"Why, mother!" Chris said.

I blushed.

"I guess it's all true about Italian men being incurably romantic," she said. "How exciting! What does the note say?"

I opened the note. It said, "A beautiful black-and-white photograph has just been taken of you and your gondola party. Prints are obtainable at five hundred lire each at the A-One Photo And Sourvenir Shop, 14 Via Nazionale."

"Here is Hotel Europa," the gondolier said, stopping the boat at the foot of a wide flight of steps leading up to a dining terrace directly above the Grand Canal.

A doorman hurried forward to help us out of the gondola, which was bobbing and lurching alarmingly in the wake of a passing motor launch. Eighty guests paused in the midst of dinner, forks in mid-air, to watch the debarkation.

"I can't," Chris said, drawing her foot back at the last minute. "I'll fall in, I know I will."

"Andiamo!" the gondolier cried gaily, giving her a little shove.

She shrieked.

"Did he pinch you?" I asked her.

"He pushed me," Chris said.

"Andiamo!" the gondolier cried again, not quite so gaily this time, and gave her another shove. At the same moment the doorman grabbed her arm and, with one last shriek, she clambered out. I followed ungracefully.

"Welcome to Venezia," the doorman said.

The center of Venice, the place you couldn't keep away from even if you wanted to, is St. Mark's Square, a phenomenon and a half. After Mark Twain puts into perspective the cathedral that gives the square its name, Irvin S. Cobb and Dorothy Kaucher look, respectively, at and from the point of view of the only inhabitant of St. Mark's Square that outnumbers the tourist.

Mark Twain
Antiquities 1880

ST. MARK IS NOT THE OLDEST building in the world, of course, but it seems the oldest, and looks the oldest—especially inside. When the ancient mosaics in its walls become damaged, they are repaired but not altered; the grotesque old pattern is preserved. Antiquity has a charm of its own, and to smarten it up would only damage it.

One day I was sitting on a red marble bench in the vestibule looking up at an ancient piece of apprentice-work, in mosaic, illustrative of the command to "multiply and replenish the earth." The Cathedral itself had seemed very old; but this picture was illustrating a period in history which made the building seem young by comparison. But I presently found an antique which was older than either the battered Cathedral or the date assigned to that piece of history; it was a spiral-shaped fossil as large as the crown of a hat; it was embedded in the marble bench, and had been sat upon by tourists until it was worn smooth. Contrasted with the inconceivable antiquity of this modest fossil, those other things were flippantly modern—jejune—mere matters of day-before-yesterday. The sense of the oldness of the Cathedral vanished away under the influence of this truly venerable presence.

Irvin S. Cobb
Day and Night 1913

THERE IS BUT ONE WAY to escape from [the shopkeepers'] everlasting persecutions, and that is to flee to the center of the square and enjoy the company of the pigeons and the photographers. They—the pigeons, I mean—belong to the oldest family in Venice; their lineage is of the purest and most undefiled. For upward of seven hundred years the authorities of the city have been feeding and protecting the pigeons, of which these countless blue-and-bronze flocks are the direct descendants. They are true aristocrats; and, like true aristocrats, they are content to live on the public funds and grow fat and sassy thereon, paying nothing in return.

No; I take that part back—they do pay something in return; a full measure. They pay by the beauty of their presence, and they are surely very beautiful, with their dainty mincing pink feet and the sheen on the proudly arched breast coverts of the cock birds; and they pay by giving you their trust and their friendship. To gobble the gifts of dried peas, which you buy in little cornucopias from convenient venders for distribution among them, they come wheeling in winged battalions, creaking and cooing, and alight on your head and shoulders in that perfect confidence which so delights humans when wild or half-wild creatures bestow it on us, though, at every opportunity, we do our level best to destroy it by hunting and harrying them to death.

At night, when the moon is up, is the time to visit this spot. Standing here, with the looming pile of the Doge's Palace bulked behind you, and the gorgeous but somewhat garish decorations of the great cathedral softened and soothed into perfection of outline and coloring by the half light, you can for the moment forget the fallen state of Venice, and your imagination peoples the splendid plaza for you with the ghosts of its dead and vanished greatnesses. You conceive of the place as it must have looked in those old, brave, wicked days, filled all with knights, with red-robed cardinals and clanking men at arms, with fair ladies and grave senators, slinking bravos and hired assassins—and all so gay with silk and satin and glittering steel and spangling gems.

By the eye of your mind you see His Illuminated Excellency, the frosted Christmas card, as he bows low before His Eminence, the pink Easter egg; you see, half hidden behind the shadowed columns of the long portico, an illustrated Sunday supplement in six colors bargaining with a stick of striped peppermint candy to have his best friend stabbed in the back before morning; you see giddy poster designs carrying on flirtations with hand-painted valentines; you catch the love-making, overhear the intriguing, and scent the plotting; you are an eyewitness to a slice out of the life of the most sinister, the most artistic, and the most murderous period of Italian history.

But by day imperious Caesar, dead and turn'd to clay, stops a hole to keep the wind away; and the wild ass of the ninety-day tour stamps his heedless hoofs over the spot where sleeps the dust of departed grandeur. By day the chug of the motor boat routs out old sleepy echoes from cracked and crannied ruins; the burnished golden frescoes of Saint Mark's blare at you as with brazen trumpets; every third medieval church has been turned into a moving-picture place; and the shopkeeping parasites buzz about you in vermin swarms and bore holes in your pocketbook until it is all one large painful welt. The emblem of Venice is the winged lion. It should be the tapeworm.

Dorothy Kaucher
From Me, A Pigeon of Venice 1960

A message to you from Venice—
I'm a pigeon of St. Mark's Square.
We pigeons are joining a union,
We think it is only fair.

We're bilious from overeating
That blasted corn that you buy.
For OUR sakes *please* vary the menu
Before we squat down and die!

We're going to take a corn break
Every afternoon at five,
And roost in the Doge's Palace
And watch YOUR swarming hive,

And throw YOU down some dried corn,
The same kind every day,
And see how YOU'd like to swallow,
And swallow without any pay.

So we're charging you 30 lira
Every time we light on your ear,
When four of us work together
We're doubling the fee, do you hear?

That nose dive for elbows is tricky,
And that goes for ears, as I said,
But the worst is that three point landing
On the top of your wobbly head.

In the night time, but you may not know it,
We fly to the Tower of the Bell,
Where we take our pigeon tum-tums
Before having another spell.

So—we're glad to pay dues to the union,
To Pigeons Protective St. Mark's,
And when we get to our heaven
Here's hoping we're skylarking larks!

One doesn't think of Henry James, an excellent travel writer in his youth and a great but serious novelist all his life, as a humorist. But the romance as well as the quantity of tourists in Venice brings out the funny or, at least, ironic bone in almost everyone. Unlike most humorists, however, James supplies a solution to the Venetian tourist's anxieties: stick around.

Henry James
Day to Day 1883

IT IS POSSIBLE TO DISLIKE VENICE, and to entertain the sentiment in a responsible and intelligent manner. There are travellers who think the place odious, and those who are not of this opinion often find themselves wishing that the others were only more numerous. The sentimental tourist's only quarrel with his Venice is that he has too many competitors there. He likes to be alone; to be original; to have (to himself, at least) the air of making discoveries. The Venice of to-day is a vast museum where the little wicket that admits you is perpetually turning and creaking, and you march through the institution with a herd of fellow-gazers. There is nothing left to discover or describe, and originality of attitude is completely impossible. This is often very annoying; you can only turn your back on your impertinent playfellow and curse his want of delicacy. But this is not the fault of Venice; it is the fault of the rest of the world. The fault of Venice is that, though it is easy to admire it, it is not so easy to live in it. After you have been there a week, and the bloom of novelty has rubbed off, you wonder whether you can accommodate yourself to the peculiar conditions. Your old habits become impracticable, and you find yourself obliged to form new ones of an undesirable and unprofitable character. You are tired of your gondola (or you think you are), and you have seen all the principal pictures and heard the names of the palaces announced a dozen times by your gondolier, who brings them out almost as impressively as if he were an English butler bawling titles into a drawing-room. You have walked several hundred times round the Piazza, and bought several bushels of photographs. You have visited the antiquity-mongers whose horrible sign-boards dishonour some of the grandest vistas in the Grand Canal; you have tried the opera and found it very bad; you have bathed at the Lido and found the water flat. You have begun to have a shipboard-feeling—to regard the Piazza as an enormous saloon and the Riva degli Schiavoni as a promenade-deck. You are obstructed and encaged; your desire for space is unsatisfied; you miss your usual exercise. You try to take a walk, and you fail, and meantime, as I say, you have come to regard your gondola as a sort of magnified baby's cradle. You have no desire to be rocked to sleep, though you are sufficiently kept awake by the irritation produced, as you gaze across the shallow lagoon, by the attitude of the perpetual gondolier, with his turned-out toes, his protruded chin, his absurdly unscientific stroke. The canals have a horrible smell, and the everlasting Piazza, where you have looked repeatedly at every article in every shop-window and found them all rubbish, where the young Venetians who sell bead-bracelets and "panoramas" are perpetually thrusting their wares at you, where the same tightly-buttoned officers are for ever sucking the same black weeds, at the same empty tables, in front of the same *caffès*—the Piazza, as I say, has resolved itself into a sort of magnificent tread-mill. This is the state of mind of those shallow inquirers who find Venice all very well for a week; and if in such a state of mind you take your departure, you act with fatal rashness. The loss is your own, moreover; it is not—with all deference to your personal attractions—that of your companions who remain behind; for though there are some disagreeable things in Venice, there is nothing so disagreeable as the visitors. The conditions are peculiar, but your intolerance of them evaporates before it has had time to become a prejudice. When you have called for the bill to go, pay it and remain, and you will find on the morrow that you are deeply attached to Venice. It is by living there from day to day that you feel the fulness of its charm; that you invite its exquisite influence to sink into your spirit. The place is as changeable as a nervous woman, and you know it only when you know all the aspects of its beauty. It has high spirits or low, it is pale or red, gray or pink, cold or warm, fresh or wan, according to the weather or the hour. It is always interesting and almost always sad; but it has a thousand occasional graces and is always liable to happy accidents. You become extraordinarily fond of these things; you count upon them; they make part of your life. Tenderly fond you become; there is something indefinable in those depths of personal acquaintance that gradually establish themselves. The place seems to personify itself, to become human and sentient, and conscious of your affection. You desire to embrace it, to caress it, to possess it; and finally, a soft sense of possession grows up, and your visit becomes a perpetual love-affair.

"Of course, one can get Italian waiters at home, but these are fresher."

Merrily Harpur

ꝼFlorence

ꝼ*Florence is a singular city. You go to Rome for Rome and to Venice for Venice, but you do not go to Florence for Florence; you go to Florence for art. For churches, sculptures, and paintings. Florence might as well be called the Florence Museum of Renaissance Art.*

Renaissance is a funny word. In the dictionary it means rebirth, but to us it means old, dead but not quite gone. Fading, perhaps, but still there for us to visit. And we do, in hordes greater than those that sacked Rome. American ironicist Russell Lynes introduces us to the great center of Western culture and British humorist Alan Brien looks at Florence in the off-season. Finally, an excerpt from E. M. Forster's novel A Room with a View, *where the essence of visiting Florence is presented through the story of two English women who nearly get lost on their way to Santa Croce Church.*

Russell Lynes
No Relief 1952

YOU SEE MORE EXHAUSTED TOURISTS in Florence, more tired limbs being rested in cafés, more noses in guidebooks, more craning necks, and more busy cameras than in any other city in Italy. There is no relief in Florence from culture but more culture. You sit in a café drinking coffee with Michelangelo's David looming above you. You dine with Giotto's campanile at your elbow. All around you is the past, the distant past; you don't find the present anywhere—unless you call motor scooters the present, but even these racketing demons somehow seem to be swallowed in the dust of antiquity. No matter what the truth of Florence's present may be with its peripheral factories and farms and its high concentration of Communists, the traveler is assailed by the feeling that all winter long the artisans of the city are preparing for his summer visit; they are busily tooling century-old designs on leather for him to take back to America, or Germany, or England, or wherever he comes from. Only in Florence did I have the conviction that if it weren't for me and for people like me—the Baedeker set—the city would crumble away into dust.

The feeling is aggravated by the fact that there are almost no surprises in Florence. Everywhere you look there is something that you have seen before—on a slide in a college art course, in a sepia photograph on your grandmother's living-room wall, on a page in your Latin grammar. You are so used to seeing these things at second hand that nothing has any reality of its own; it looks only like a reproduction of itself.

This, of course, is a superficial and probably prejudiced view. You do find unexpected sights to arrest your vision, but the eye slides over the Ghiberti bapistry doors ("The Gates of Paradise") as easily as they slide over the buildings of a familiar street at home. You find yourself in a room in the Uffizi filled with Botticellis. Here is the "Primavera" and here is "The Birth of Venus." You say to yourself that you ought to be impressed; what are you here for anyway? But how can you pretend to affect an emotion for these second-hand acquaintances of your childhood when you know quite well that it has been years since you have bothered to look at the excellent Botticelli in your local museum? So you wander on, mentally ticking off masterpieces on your checklist. The pictures that stop you in your tracks as you traipse from room to room are fewer than you expected and they are usually not the ones you came to see. They are the ones you had forgotten were there, if you ever knew, or ones you never heard of.

On the ship going to Italy I met an archæologist who said, "I don't remember ever having spent a happy hour in Florence." I, who had never been there, put that down to an archæologist's prejudice against a living civilization. But I came to see what he meant. Florence is neither quite dead and on the dissecting table, nor is it quite alive; it is in a coma from which one suspects it will never awaken. Its scarcely breathing but beautiful body lies at the bottom of a valley surrounded by a garland of hills dotted with pleasant villas; and through its narrow streets swarm a horde of gate crashers four hundred years too late for the party.

Alan Brien
Tuscan Columns 1985

WE HAD BORROWED a third-floor, two-room flat in one of the oldest quarters, behind the Teatro Verdi, across the road from Santa Croce. We were within five minutes' walk of more antique statues, wall-size Old Masters, vistas of umber and gold and sepia perspectives, marble squares and terracotta towers, fortresses that could have been chipped out of old cork, Babylonian roof gardens, cavernous apothecary's shops like Etruscan temples, pavements hand-laid in individually baked bricks, than would seem convincing if we had been born, and raised, in the British Museum. Yet the other city in which I have lived that came to mind on waking each morning was New York.

As your eyes opened the light filtered down from above, bouncing, bending, taking on tints and shades as it sank, like a shower of glass rods in an aquarium. It was worse than guesswork to estimate the cold of the sky and the state of the weather from the pattern on the window. Even leaning out, and squinting up, was little help unless you could spot a small geometrical shape of sunshine far away among the chimney tops.

The contrast between eternally chilly depths and gradually warmed externals may be what keeps the winds on their toes. Certainly, hardly a Florentine is to be seen unprotected by the impervious, malleable armour of some other creature's skin. The women are all in furs, the men all in leather. After a few days during which the cover dropped on the parrot's cage, bringing with it the boisterous, blood-chilling dark, around four in the afternoon, I began to regard the citizens less with righteous disapproval than with selfish envy.

There seemed to be no occasion, inside almost as often as outside, where the fur coat did not rate as regular wear. I saw women bicycling in furs, usually in the wrong direction down a one-way street and into the pedestrian precinct. (In Italy, the bike has all the rights of a citizen on foot and ignores traffic laws for vehicles. But then, at least in Naples and the south, I was solemnly informed that the red light was not an order to anybody but more in the way of a bit of friendly advice.) I saw women in furs cutting up fish in the market, carrying loads of newspapers into shops, sweeping out courtyards, breast-feeding the baby on the bus.

What I did not notice, in my glazed male way, was that the fur coat was a many-patterned uniform, regimented according to rank. Once you had learned the signs, you could identify the class of every Florentine female. This was demonstrated to me by a city resident of cosmopolitan origin. Wherever we were, she would say something like "See, that is the daughter. She is wearing the top level working-class fur. But she is with her mother-in-law who demonstrates her dominance by wearing the bottom level middle-class fur."

The leather of the attendant male kept pace, though in rather more subtle fashion which it took me longer to spot, usually restricting the fur to a lining. An exception was pointed out in the Via de Tornabuoni, a shopping arcade commonly described as "the Bond Street of Florence" though, to me, a dedicated non-shopper, it seemed far superior as a theatrical show-case, a display of conspicuous commercialism presented with electrifying style.

Here were a couple, probably in their late sixties, identically dressed in a soft, neat patchwork of pinky-grey fur from high-collared neck to Gucci bootees, heads topped with fluffy turbans of the same dead creatures. My guide estimated they were carrying on their backs the price of a sizable luxury flat, probably in the Tornabuoni. And so did every other passer-by. Which was the point of the exercise.

E.M. Forster
In Santa Croce with
No Baedeker 1923

IT WAS PLEASANT TO WAKE UP IN FLORENCE, to open the eyes upon a bright bare room, with a floor of red tiles which look clean though they are not; with a painted ceiling whereon pink griffins and blue amorini sport in a forest of yellow violins and bassoons. It was pleasant, too, to fling wide the windows, pinching the fingers in unfamiliar fastenings, to lean out into sunshine with beautiful hills and trees and marble churches opposite, and close below, the Arno, gurgling against the embankment of the road.

Over the river men were at work with spades and sieves on the sandy foreshore, and on the river was a boat, also diligently employed for some mysterious end. An electric tram came rushing underneath the window.

No one was inside it, except one tourist; but its platforms were overflowing with Italians, who preferred to stand. Children tried to hang on behind, and the conductor, with no malice, spat in their faces to make them let go. Then soldiers appeared—good-looking, undersized men—wearing each a knapsack covered with mangy fur, and a great-coat which had been cut for some larger soldier. Beside them walked officers, looking foolish and fierce, and before them went little boys, turning somersaults in time with the band. The tramcar became entangled in their ranks, and moved on painfully, like a caterpillar in a swarm of ants. One of the little boys fell down, and some white bullocks came out of an archway. Indeed, if it had not been for the good advice of an old man who was selling button-hooks, the road might never have got clear.

Over such trivialities as these many a valuable hour may slip away, and the traveller who has gone to Italy to study the tactile values of Giotto, or the corruption of the Papacy, may return remembering nothing but the blue sky and the men and women who live under it. So it was as well that Miss Bartlett should tap and come in, and having commented on Lucy's leaving the door unlocked, and on her leaning out of the window before she was fully dressed, should urge her to hasten herself, or the best of the day would be gone. By the time Lucy was ready her cousin had done her breakfast, and was listening to the clever lady among the crumbs.

A conversation then ensued, on not unfamiliar lines. Miss Bartlett was, after all, a wee bit tired, and thought they had better spend the morning settling in; unless Lucy would at all like to go out? Lucy would rather like to go out, as it was her first day in Florence, but, of course, she could go alone. Miss Bartlett could not allow this. Of course she would accompany Lucy everywhere. Oh, certainly not; Lucy would stop with her cousin. Oh, no! that would never do. Oh, yes!

At this point the clever lady broke in.

"If it is Mrs. Grundy who is troubling you, I do assure you that you can neglect the good person. Being English, Miss Honeychurch will be perfectly safe. Italians understand. A dear friend of mine, Contessa Baroncelli, has two daughters, and when she cannot send a maid to school with them, she lets them go in sailor-hats instead. Every one takes them for English, you see, especially if their hair is strained tightly behind."

Miss Bartlett was unconvinced by the safety of Contessa Baroncelli's daughters. She was determined to take Lucy herself, her head not being so very bad. The clever lady then said that she was going to spend a long morning in Santa Croce, and if Lucy would come too, she would be delighted.

"I will take you by a dear dirty back way, Miss Honeychurch, and if you bring me luck, we shall have an adventure."

Lucy said that this was most kind, and at once opened the Baedeker, to see where Santa Croce was.

"Tut, tut! Miss Lucy! I hope we shall soon emancipate you from Baedeker. He does but touch the surface of things. As to the true Italy—he does not even dream of it. The true Italy is only to be found by patient observation."

This sounded very interesting, and Lucy hurried over her breakfast, and started with her new friend in high spirits. Italy was coming at last. * * *

Miss Lavish—for that was the clever lady's name—turned to the right along the sunny Lung' Arno. How delightfully warm! But a wind down the side streets cut like a knife, didn't it? Ponte alle Grazie—particularly interesting, mentioned by Dante. San Miniato—beautiful as well as interesting; the crucifix that kissed a murderer—Miss Honeychurch would remember the story. The men on the river were fishing. (Untrue; but then, so is most information.) Then Miss Lavish darted under the archway of the white bullocks, and she stopped, and she cried:

"A smell! a true Florentine smell! Every city, let me teach you, has its own smell."

"Is it a very nice smell?" said Lucy, who had inherited from her mother a distaste to dirt.

"One doesn't come to Italy for niceness," was the retort; "one comes for life. *Buon giorno! Buon giorno!*" bowing right and left. "Look at that adorable wine-cart! How the driver stares at us, dear, simple soul!"

So Miss Lavish proceeded through the streets of the city of Florence, short, fidgety, and playful as a kitten, though without a kitten's grace. It was a treat for the girl to be with any one so clever and so cheerful; and a blue military cloak, such as an Italian officer wears, only increased the sense of festivity.

"*Buon giorno!* Take the word of an old woman, Miss Lucy: you will never repent of a little civility to your inferiors. *That* is the true democracy. Though I am a real Radical as well. There, now you're shocked."

"Indeed, I'm not!" exclaimed Lucy. "We are Radicals, too, out and out. My father always voted for Mr. Gladstone, until he was so dreadful about Ireland."

"I see, I see. And now you have gone over to the enemy."

"Oh, please—! If my father was alive, I am sure he would vote Radical again now that Ireland is all right. And as it is, the glass over our front-door was broken last election, and Freddy is sure it was the Tories; but mother says nonsense, a tramp."

"Shameful! A manufacturing district, I suppose?"

"No—in the Surrey hills. About five miles from Dorking, looking over the Weald."

Miss Lavish seemed interested, and slackened her trot.

"What a delightful part; I know it so well. It is full of the very nicest people. Do you know Sir Harry Otway—a Radical if every there was?"

"Very well indeed."

"And old Mrs. Butterworth the philanthropist?"

"Why, she rents a field of us! How funny!"

Miss Lavish looked at the narrow ribbon of sky, and murmured:

"Oh, you have property in Surrey?"

"Hardly any," said Lucy, fearful of being thought a snob. "Only thirty acres—just the garden, all downhill, and some fields."

Miss Lavish was not disgusted, and said it was just the size of her aunt's Suffolk estate. Italy receded. They tried to remember the last name of Lady Louisa some one, who had taken a house near Summer Street the other year, but she had not liked it, which was odd of her. And just as Miss Lavish had got the name, she broke off and exclaimed:

"Bless us! Bless us and save us! We've lost the way."

Certainly they had seemed a long time in reaching Santa Croce, the tower of which had been plainly visible from the landing window. But Miss Lavish had said so much about knowing her Florence by heart, that Lucy had followed her with no misgivings.

"Lost! lost! My dear Miss Lucy, during our political diatribes we have taken a wrong turning. How those horrid Conservatives would jeer at us! What are we to do? Two lone females in an unknown town. Now, this is what *I* call an adventure."

Lucy, who wanted to see Santa Croce, suggested, as a possible solution, that they should ask the way there.

"Oh, but that is the word of a craven! And no, you are not, not, *not* to look at your Baedeker. Give it to me; I shan't let you carry it. We will simply drift."

Accordingly they drifted through a series of those grey-brown streets, neither commodious nor picturesque, in which the eastern quarter of the city abounds. Lucy soon lost interest in the discontent of Lady Louisa, and became discontented herself. For one ravishing moment Italy appeared. She stood in the Square of the Annunziata and saw in the living terra-cotta those divine babies whom no cheap reproduction can ever stale. There they stood, with their shining limbs bursting from the garments of charity, and their strong white arms extended against circlets of heaven. Lucy thought she had never seen anything more beautiful; but Miss Lavish, with a shriek of dismay, dragged her forward, declaring that they were out of their path now by at least a mile.

The hour was approaching at which the continental breakfast begins, or rather ceases, to tell, and the ladies bought some hot chestnut paste out of a little shop, because it looked so typical. It tasted partly of the paper in which it was wrapped, partly of hair oil, partly of the great unknown. But it gave them strength to drift into another Piazza, large and dusty, on the farther side of which rose a black-and-white facade of surpassing ugliness. Miss Lavish spoke to it dramatically. It was Santa Croce. The adventure was over.

"Stop a minute; let those two people go on, or I shall have to speak to them. I do detest conventional intercourse. Nasty! they are going into the church, too. Oh, the Britisher abroad!"

"We sat opposite them at dinner last night. They have given us their rooms. They were so very kind."

"Look at their figures!" laughed Miss Lavish. "They walk through my Italy like a pair of cows. It's very naughty of me, but I would like to set an examination paper at Dover, and turn back every tourist who couldn't pass it."

"What would you ask us?"

Miss Lavish laid her hand pleasantly on Lucy's arm, as if to suggest that she, at all events, would get full marks. In this exalted mood they reached the steps of the great church....

Go to Rome

*A*lthough I have here, dear reader—the Brera and Ambrosiana being in my way—a glorious opportunity to serve up views on art, I will still suffer this cup to pass away from you, contenting myself with the remark that I have observed the pointed chin, which gives such a sentimental impression to so many pictures of the Lombard school, on many a pretty Lombardess in the streets of Milan. It has always been marvelously comforting and edifying to me when an opportunity presented itself to compare the works of a school with the originals which served as its models; for thus I more accurately appreciated its character. Thus in the great fair of Rotterdam, the divine geniality of Jan Steen was suddenly revealed to me; and thus at a later date I learned on Lung l'Arno the truth of form and the effective spirit of the Florentines, while in San Marco I caught the truth of color and the dreamy superficiality of the Venetians. Go to Rome, my dear soul—go to Rome—and there perhaps you may rise to a perception of the ideal and to the appreciation of Raphael. *—Heinrich Heine, 1824*

"We must be in the Italian Alps."

❧Activities

❧*It is Italy's art treasures that are its biggest draw, that is, the ones that haven't been sold or stolen. People who rarely visit the Italian treasures in their local museums spend thousands of hard-earned dollars and pounds in a crash-course in Culture, with the most capital of capital C's. The guidebooks are generally excellent on telling you things you wouldn't dream of asking about specific schools and works of art, but it takes humorists like Arthur Maquarie, Laurie Taylor, and, to lead things off, the master of Masters, Mark Twain, to strip off the layers of soot and reveal the truth about Italian art and its importance to the tourist.*

Mark Twain
The Old Masters 1880

WE VISITED THE PICTURE GALLERIES and the other regulation "sights" of Milan—not because I wanted to write about them again, but to see if I had learned anything in twelve years. I afterwards visited the great galleries of Rome and Florence for the same purpose. I found I had learned one thing. When I wrote about the Old Masters before, I said the copies were better than the originals. That was a mistake of large dimensions. The Old Masters were still unpleasing to me, but they were truly divine contrasted with the copies. The copy is to the original as the pallid, smart, inane new wax work-group is to the vigorous, earnest, dignified group of living men and women whom it professes to duplicate. There is a mellow richness, a subdued color, in the old pictures, which is to the eye what muffled and mellowed sound is to the ear. That is the merit which is most loudly praised in the old picture, and is the one which the copy most conspicuously lacks, and which the copyist must not hope to compass. It was generally conceded by the artists with whom I talked, that that subdued splendor, that mellow richness, is imparted to the picture by age. Then why should we worship the Old Master for it, who didn't impart it, instead of worshiping Old Time, who did? Perhaps the picture was a clanging bell, until Time muffled it and sweetened it.

In conversation with an artist in Venice, I asked—

"What is it that people see in the Old Masters? I have been in the Doge's Palace and I saw several acres of very bad drawing, very bad perspective, and very incorrect proportions. Paul Veronese's dogs do not resemble dogs; all the horses look like bladders on legs; one man had a right leg on the left side of his body; in the large picture where the Emperor (Barbarossa?) is prostrate before the Pope, there are three men in the foreground who are over thirty feet high, if one may judge by the size of a kneeling little boy in the centre of the foreground; and according to the same scale, the Pope is 7 feet high and the Doge is a shriveled dwarf of 4 feet."

The artist said—

"Yes, the Old Masters often drew badly; they did not care much for truth and exactness in minor details; but after all, in spite of bad drawing, bad perspective, bad proportions, and a choice of subjects which no longer appeal to people as strongly as they did three hundred years ago, there is a something about their pictures which is divine—a something which is above and beyond the art of any epoch since—a something which would be the despair of artists but that they never hope or expect to attain it, and therefore do not worry about it."

That is what he said—and he said what he believed; and not only believed, but felt.

Reasoning—especially reasoning without technical knowledge—must be put aside, in cases of this kind. It cannot assist the inquirer. It will lead him, in the most logical progression, to what, in the eyes of artists, would be a most illogical conclusion. Thus: bad drawing, bad proportion, bad perspective, indifference to truthful detail, color which gets its merit from time, and not from the artist—these things constitute the Old Master; conclusion, the Old Master was a bad painter, the Old Master was not an Old Master at all, but an Old Apprentice. Your friend the artist will grant your premises, but deny your conclusion; he will maintain that notwithstanding this formidable list of confessed defects, there is still a something that is divine and unapproachable about the Old Master, and that there is no arguing the fact away by any system of reasoning whatever.

I can believe that. There are women who have an indefinable charm in their faces which makes them beautiful to their intimates; but a cold stranger who tried to reason the matter out and find this beauty would fail. He would say of one of these women: this chin is too short, this nose is too long, this forehead is too high, this hair is too red, this complexion is too pallid, the perspective of the entire composition is incorrect; conclusion, the woman is not beautiful. But her nearest friend might say, and say truly, "Your premises are right, your logic is faultless, but your conclusion is wrong, nevertheless; she is an Old Master—she is beautiful, but only to such as know her; it is a beauty which cannot be formulated, but it is there just the same."

I found more pleasure in contemplating the Old Masters this time than I did when I was in Europe in former years, but still it was a calm pleasure; there was nothing over-heated about it. When I was in Venice before, I think I found no picture which stirred me much, but this time there were two which enticed me to the Doge's Palace day after day, and kept me there hours at a time. One of these was Tintoretto's three-acre picture in the Great Council Chamber. When I saw it 12 years ago I was not strongly attracted to it—the guide told me it was an insurrection in heaven—but this was an error. * * *

The other great work which fascinated me was Bassano's immortal Hair Trunk. This is in the Chamber of the Council of Ten. It is in one of the three forty-foot pictures which decorate the walls of the room. The composition of this picture is beyond praise. The Hair Trunk is not hurled at the stranger's head—so to speak—as the chief feature of an immortal work so often is; no, it is carefully guarded from prominence, it is subordinated, it is restrained, it is most deftly and cleverly held in reserve, it is most cautiously and ingeniously led up to, by the master, and consequently when the spectator reaches it at last, he is taken unawares, he is unprepared, and it bursts upon him with a stupefying surprise.

One is lost in wonder at all the thought and care which this elaborate planning must have cost. A general glance at the picture could never suggest that there was a hair trunk in it; the Hair Trunk is not mentioned in the title even—which is, "Pope Alexander III and the Doge Ziani, the Conqueror of the Emperor Frederick Barbarossa;" you see, the title is actually utilized to help divert attention from the Trunk; thus, as I say, nothing suggests the presence of the Trunk, by any hint, yet everything studiedly leads up to it, step by step. Let us examine into this, and observe the exquisitely artful artlessness of the plan.

At the extreme left end of the picture are a couple of women, one of them with a child looking over her shoulder at a wounded man sitting with bandaged head on the ground. These people seem needless, but no, they are there for a purpose; one cannot look at them without seeing the gorgeous procession of grandees, bishops, halberdiers, and banner-bearers which is passing along behind them; one cannot see the procession without feeling a curiosity to follow it and learn whither it is going; it leads him to the Pope, in the center of the picture, who is talking with the bonnetless Doge—talking tranquilly, too, although within 12 feet of them a man is beating a drum, and not far from the drummer two persons are blowing horns, and many horsemen are plunging and rioting about—indeed, 22 feet of this great work is all a deep and happy holiday serenity and Sunday School procession, and then we come suddenly upon 11 1/2 feet of turmoil and racket and insubordination. This latter state of things is not an accident, it has its purpose. But for it, one would linger upon the Pope and the Doge, thinking them to be the motive and supreme feature of the picture; whereas one is drawn along, almost unconsciously, to see what the trouble is about. Now at the very *end* of this riot, within 4 feet of the end of the picture, and full 36 feet from the beginning of it, the Hair Trunk bursts with an electrifying suddenness upon the spectator, in all its matchless perfection, and the great master's triumph is sweeping and complete. From that moment no other thing in those forty feet of canvas has any charm; one sees the Hair Trunk, and the Hair Trunk only—and to see it is to worship it. Bassano even placed objects in the immediate vicinity of the Supreme Feature whose pretended purpose was to divert attention from it yet a little longer and thus delay and augment the surprise; for instance, to the right of it he has placed a stooping man with a cap so red that it is sure to hold the eye for a moment—to the left of it, some 6 feet away, he has placed a red-coated man on an inflated horse, and that coat plucks your eye to that locality the next moment—then, between the Trunk and the red horseman he has intruded a man, naked to his waist, who is carrying a fancy flour sack on the middle of his back instead of on his shoulder—this admirable feat interests you, of course—keeps you at bay a little longer, like a sock or a jacket thrown to the pursuing wolf—but at last, in spite of all distractions and detentions, the eye of even the most dull and heedless spectator is sure to fall upon the World's Masterpiece, and in that moment he totters to his chair or leans upon his guide for support.

Descriptions of such a work as this must necessarily be imperfect, yet they are of value. The top of the Trunk is arched; the arch is a perfect half circle, in the Roman style of architecture, for in the then rapid decadence of Greek art, the rising influence of Rome was already beginning to be felt in the art of the Republic. The Trunk is bound or bordered with leather all around where the lid joins the main body. Many critics consider this leather too cold in tone; but I consider this its highest merit, since it was evidently made so to emphasize by contrast the impassioned fervor of the hasp. The high lights in part of the work are cleverly managed, the *motif* is admirably subordinated to the ground tints, and the *technique* is very fine. The brass nail-heads are in the purest style of the early renaissance. The strokes, here, are very firm and bold—every nail-head is a portrait. The handle on the end of the Trunk has evidently been retouched—I think, with a piece of chalk—but one can still see the inspiration of the Old Master in the tranquil, almost too tranquil, hang of it. The hair of this Trunk is *real* hair—so to speak—white in patches, brown in patches. The details are finely worked out; the repose proper to hair in a recumbent and inactive attitude is charmingly expressed. There is a feeling about this part of the work which lifts it to the highest altitudes of art; the sense of sordid realism vanishes away—one recognizes that there is *soul* here. View this Trunk as you will, it is a gem, it is a marvel, it is a miracle. Some of the effects are very daring, approaching even to the boldest flights of the rococo, the sirocco, and the Byzantine schools—yet the master's hand never falters—it moves on, calm, majestic, confident—and with that art which conceals art, it finally casts over the *tout ensemble*, by mysterious methods of its own, a subtle something which refines, subdues, etherealizes the arid components and endues them with the deep charm and gracious witchery of poesy.

Among the art treasures of Europe there are pictures which approach the Hair Trunk—there are two which may be said to equal it, possibly—but there is none that surpasses it. So perfect is the Hair Trunk that it moves even persons who ordinarily have no feeling for art. When an Erie baggage master saw it two years ago, he could hardly keep from checking it; and once when a customs inspector was brought into its presence, he gazed upon it in silent rapture for some moments, then slowly and unconsciously placed one hand behind him with the palm uppermost, and got out his chalk with the other. These facts speak for themselves.

Arthur Maquarie
B Is for Botticelli

B is for Botticelli, a crazy sort of man,
Who like many at the moment when the pagan
    craze began,
Confused Saint Paul and Socrates, and muddled
    gods and saints
Till he drew a Virgin Mary with his box of Venus
    paints.
There is something very lovely in his easy, flow-
    ing grace,
And his airiness of fancy and his gentleness of
    face,
The softness of his colours, and his evident delight

In catching pretty contours, and in getting most
    things right.
Friend Berenson has shown us—and we bow and
    hearken dumb—
He prefers an ample earlobe and a squarish type
    of thumb;
And any girl will tell you he was artful in his ways
When he made his rapt Madonnas wear their hair
    like Edna May's.

Laurie Taylor
Culture Vulture Shock 1986

I'M SORRY, GEOFF, BUT let's get this crystal clear. Are
you accusing me of actually *saying* that? You're saying
that I *said* that?"

"I don't know about you saying it, but you certainly
implied as much."

"Look, Geoff, don't give me 'implied'. A minute ago
you said 'said'. That's a very different matter from
'implied', isn't it?"

"Well, you as good as *said* it. Put it like that."

"No, I'm sorry, Geoff. You've gone a little too far this
time. I want to hear what other people think about all
this. Put it to the vote. Did anyone here—anyone at all in
our group—ever hear me say that Jacopo Tintoretto was
without doubt the supreme Renaissance colourist? Did
anyone ever hear me say that?"

Although there were eight of us sitting around the table
at the well-located Pensione Salute, dipping our after-
dinner grapes in the now pleasantly tepid bowl of water,
not one of us could quite remember Alex coming out with
those exact words.

"What I *did* say, and it was on about the second day of
last year's holiday, just after we'd been bargaining with
that man outside the Accademia about the price of the
melon slices— '*cocomero*', remember?—what I said, then,

was that Tintoretto was arguably the Renaissance master of *chiaroscuro*, of light and shade, that is. Light and shade. Right, Geoff? Not colour. There is a difference, you know."

You could feel that the atmosphere was becoming charged, and although most of us were still in a contented mood after a fine meal of minestrone, liver (Venetian style), and *zuppa inglese*, I, for one, was pleased that Christine stopped peeling her grapes for a second and tried to introduce some sense of proportion into the proceedings.

"Look, do stop it, you two, I mean, what's the point of falling out over details, over who said exactly what, and to whom. We're all Tintoretto people, aren't we?"

I could see that her appeal had got through to Geoff. He switched his eyes away from Alex and took a large reflective sip from his *acqua minerale* glass.

"I mean, everybody here recognises that Tintoretto's footsteps are all over Venice and that the sheer power and vitality of his imagination was unparalleled by any of his contemporaries. Yes?"

"Yes," muttered Geoff.

"And surely everyone here would agree that he worked like a giant, flinging himself 'upon the wings of all the winds'?"

Most of us nodded.

"So why, for goodness sake, spoil the evening with such pointless bickering?"

Of course, in a way, it was easy for Christine to talk. Not only had she steered clear of the Barolo that evening because such heavy red wine tended to aggravate her mosquito bites, but she's also been in the South Manchester Tintoretto group ever since that rainy day at the Lido back in 1976 when a small group of people sheltering together in a tiny beach-hut had decided to do something in their own way to counter Paul Theroux's interesting but sweeping generalisation that "travel, so broadening at first" eventually "contracts the mind".

Compared to Christine, Alex and Geoff were virtual newcomers to cultural vacations: Alex coming over to us from a primarily Oldham-based Carpaccio group in 1983 when he felt it was taking a slightly too sentimental view of Gentile Bellini, and Geoff only deserting the Didsbury Titian society in 1984 after a ridiculous argument one night in St. Mark's Square about the exact symbolic significance of the old woman with the eggs in the *Presentation*.

"Look, do me a favour, Christine." Whatever Geoff's view of the matter it was instantly clear that Alex was anxious to return to the fray. "No one needs your help. Our friend Geoff here is positively looking for a little aggro. Am I right, Geoffrey?"

"I don't know what you're talking about. I really don't. I only took up a remark which you yourself made less than twelve months ago..."

"I think you do, old son. I think you do. I've been watching you very carefully this holiday. There have been little signs. Last Monday, for example, when you slipped out of San Rocco just as we were getting down to some detailed work on the top left hand corner of *Paradiso*."

"Only because I had to get some antihistamine before the chemist's..."

"And then on Tuesday I caught you giggling in front of *Cain and Abel*."

"Well, there is something a little disconcerting about the way they're..."

"And now there's all this chunter about the significance of colour. What next, Geoffrey, old boy? A few casual references to the distinctive qualities of *The Madonna of the Pesaro*?"

Even in the candlelight it was clear that Geoff had started to blush at Alex's reference.

"I don't know what you're talking about," he blurted, clumsily tipping the dregs of the *acqua minerale* bottle into his *grappa* glass.

"Or perhaps *The Frari Assumption?*"

"I've never mentioned the merits of *The Frari Assumption* in your presence, and you know it."

"I'm on to you, Geoffrey Tremlett. Oh yes, although you've been sitting around with us for the last two weeks, licking your chocolate *gelati*, sipping your lemon *spremutas*, and going on like everyone else about how the lavish power with which Tintoretto treats every subject cannot but fail to impress the beholder, you haven't changed your spots at all. I know where your loyalty lies. You're still a Titian man."

"I admit there are certain things that he did well. I mean, most experts would agree that his power of portraiture was unsurpassed."

"Don't give me 'certain things that he did well'. *Titian?* Are we talking about Titian? Then perhaps you'd be so good as to tell me who it was who turned the young Tintoretto out of his studio? Who it was who threw this 15-year-old raw genius on to the streets whence he was forced to search out each and every occasion for the exercise of his prodigious talent?"

"That's out of order, Alex, and you damned well know it. Tintoretto was far from blameless in the encounter. The dyer's son was often carried away by the violence and extravagance of his own imagination, by, in a word, his *spirito stravagante.*"

"A 'violence and extravagance', which you know only too well, Geoffrey Tremlett, was the driving force behind such acknowledged masterpieces as *Moses Receiving the Tablets of the Law* and *The Last Judgement.*"

"It's a pity, then, that for all their mastery of composition, such pictures singularly fail to convey any profound sense of human feeling or compassion across the centuries."

79

"I'm sorry, Geoff, but that's the last straw. That's it. Quite enough for one day. Let's settle this outside."

"Oh, that's fine. Nothing you old Carpaccio people like better than simple narrative solutions to transcendental issues."

"OUTSIDE."

"RIGHT."

It was a thoroughly nasty moment, one indeed which might have marred our entire cultural vacation, had not Christine, at that very moment, spotted through the blinds a group of youths making their way down our *calle.*

"Geoff. Alex. Everybody," she whispered putting her hand over the water bowl to block off the distraction of the remaining grapes. "Outside. By the pleasantly quiet small canal. It's the Giorgione mob."

That was more than enough for most of us. We were on our feet in an instant, and with Alex bawling "quasi-mystical bastards" at the top of his voice, and Geoff leading us all in a chorus of "Here We Go", we chased them half a mile along the Fondamenta to Ruskin's House where, with a pleasantly renewed sense of our own solidarity, we linked arms and chanted *"Raphael Raphael,"* outside the proprietor's window until it was time for bed.

❧ *Well, enough for the arts. Man cannot live by arts alone, especially while on vacation. There are so many other things to do in Italy than to get neckaches looking up at campaniles, footaches walking over too many marble floors, and headaches trying to remember who was who and what was what. We all must do our duty and see a minimum of one cathedral, two churches, three museums, and four car/vespa accidents in each town we visit, but then our time is free to do what we really want to do: eat, shop, find the most romantic hotel room, and fall in love. Three travel writers from three different generations— Sean O'Faolain, John Gibbons, and Charles Dickens—-*

introduce us to dining in the Italian ristorante, *the home of pasta, risotto, polenta, calamari, and something they call pizza. And don't forget the* vino!

Sean O'Faolain
The Casual Wanderer 1950

THE SYSTEMATIC TRAVELLER, unlike the casual traveller, has, I believe, more to record than to remember. The casual wanderer stays here, ambles there for each moment's pleasure, and afterwards when people ask him 'What did you do?' he cannot reply. The things that made him happy are too little, too evanescent, too personal to be named. I have no idea now why I wandered up so often to that restaurant on Monte Cappuccini. But over and over again I foresee that I shall have no idea about many such caprices that were, at the time, delightful to indulge. I used to read there, doze there, write there, not go down into the city until the late afternoon, when the swallows were whirling above the vine-trellis over my head. I was often the sole person to take lunch, usually ham with melon, a heap of *maccheroni napolitano*, tomatoes in olive oil, bread, butter, black olives and a white wine, for about 650 lire, then around seven shillings.

&*Italy is also the home of the memorable waiter, who fulfills your every request as skillfully as any genie, and of the celebrity maître d', a man who seeks to rise above his craft and make it into an art. And then there are the waiters who are memorable for other reasons altogether.*

John Gibbons
What I'd Really Like 1932

ALL THIS TIME I WAS NATURALLY getting hungry again, and there was no restaurant-car on this train, even if I had had the money to use it. For the Italian traveller, of course, it is easy enough. At most of the big stations there is a boy with a barrow, and their railway refreshment-rooms are more like small shops than mere bars. So that at every stop you will find a little dash of passengers to the drinking-water tap or else to the buffet to buy up provender. And in they come again with a little store of a half-bottle of wine and a loaf of bread and perhaps some sausage stuff and an orange or two. Only it makes it a bit awkward if one knows none of the Italian words to ask for. There is *pane* for bread, and *byrrha* means beer (I found that out fairly early), and then there is a stuff called *salami* that I once met in a London restaurant—and, by the way, intensely disliked. But barring a cup of black coffee for breakfast somewhere, I had practically to live on *salami* and *pane* and *byrrha* almost all the long way to Naples. This travelling-third-class business has its drawbacks.

There was one big place where we stopped quite a while, and where I hoped for some real food. But owing to a queer little incident, it did not materialise. It is possible, of course, that I exaggerate its importance, but at the time, robbed as I was of my hours-overdue meal, I felt that the business was of colossal interest.

It was a biggish station with a real refreshment-room with chairs and tables, and the moment I sat down one of the waiters came up to me and in quite capital English asked what I would like. And taken in for the moment, I rubbed my hands and told him that "anything fairly meaty" would do. "Good," he said, "the Signor wishes milk." And off he trotted over to the bar place, where several of his fellow-waiters seemed to be watching him.

So incredible appeared the outrage that I did not stop him. My ears, I thought, must have deceived me. But a minute later back he came, beaming all over his face, and carrying on a little tray an enormous glass of milk. And just at the moment that I was going to tell him exactly what I thought about people who pretended to speak a language when they really could not understand a single word of it, and exactly what he could do with his milk, I happened to glance up and catch his eyes full. He was not beaming now at all, but looked anxious, a bit like a dog that thinks he has done something wrong and is not sure what: only he is going to be punished. I suppose that I must be an imaginative ass, but in the fraction of a second that I sat there staring at the lad's face (for he was not a very old waiter) I seemed to see all sorts of things in his eyes.

There was a girl, I know, and would she ever get married now? And some little children, and would they ever be born? And a tiny little restaurant somewhere, the very pride of this lad's heart. And, so it seemed to me, the whole of everything in the world hung precariously on me: my choice as to what I did with that beastly milk. And over his shoulder I could see the other waiters still staring at our corner.

It all happened within an instant. He had not even got his tray down on my table, and his hand seemed poised in a sort of everlasting hesitation of awful anxiety. Over-imagination on my part, I suppose. Anyway, the feeling affected me so powerfully that with an effort I motioned him to put his awful milk down, and said "Thank you," and even took a shuddering sip of the stuff. And as if relieved from some tremendous burden, he almost ran back to his counter, and stood there watching me. And a moment later there came across the floor a manager gentleman who spoke real English, and what was it, please, that I had truly wanted?

As I hesitated a second, he told me that he understood the little comedy quite well. A blunder, of course, of Peppino's, and he infinitely regretted it. Let me tell him now—and he reached for the menu card—what it was I would really like, and the error should instantly be rectified. But, I said, it was milk that I wanted, and what was there to rectify? And then Mr. Manager, late of one of the great London hotels, went on. I must not think, he told me, that Peppino would get into any trouble over it. He was, indeed, a very good lad, attentive and patient, and ever so anxious to learn English and make himself a better waiter still. Only at present he had not progressed far with his lessons. By and by, perhaps. But in the meantime it was impossible that he could be allowed to misinterpret the orders of foreigners. Other *signori* might not be equally complacent. Let me say, now, what I might really like. A beef-steak, for instance?

Only with a mulish obstinacy I stuck to my milk. For, having told a lie, in fact, one might as well go on to make a thoroughly artistic job of the business. And so to the sympathetic manager I put up a rather pathetic case. One would not, of course, wish to have it mentioned everywhere, but, as he could perhaps see, at forty-seven my figure was changing. To restore it to its youthful contours a diet was necessary, and my doctor had made a definite point of no meat in the middle of the day. I had, in fact, before leaving home made a promise to my wife upon the point. And he could understand now why, hesitating before temptation, I had ordered Peppino to bring me milk. And Mr. Manager did understand the delicacy of the situation, and with a few remarks upon the London of twenty years earlier departed with many bowings. But as, the infernal stuff finished, I left the place, I thought that Peppino bowed lower still. Of course the whole thing may have been all my fancy. But, anyway, I do hope that he married the girl.

Charles Dickens
Lord Byron Ate Here 1844

BOLOGNA BEING VERY FULL of tourists, detained there by an inundation which rendered the road to Florence impassable, I was quartered up at the top of an hotel, in an out of the way room which I never could find; containing a bed, big enough for a boarding-school, which I couldn't fall asleep in. The chief among the waiters who visited this lonely retreat, where there was no other company but the swallows in the broad eaves over the window, was a man of one idea in connection with the English; and the subject of this harmless monomania was Lord Byron. I made the discovery by accidentally remarking to him, at breakfast, that the matting with which the floor was covered was very comfortable at that season, when he immediately replied that Milor Beeron had been much attached to that kind of matting. Observing, at the same moment, that I took no milk, he exclaimed, with enthusiasm, that Milor Beeron had never touched it. At first, I took it for granted, in my innocence, that he had been one of the Beeron servants; but no, he said no, he was in the habit of speaking about my Lord to English gentlemen; that was all. He knew all about him, he said. In proof of it, he connected him with every possible topic, from the Monte Pulciano wine at dinner (which was grown on an estate he had owned), to the big bed itself, which was the very model of his. When I left the inn, he coupled with his final bow in the yard a parting assurance that the road by which I was going had been Milor Beeron's favorite ride; and before the horse's feet had well begun to clatter on the pavement, he ran briskly up stairs again, I dare say to tell some other Englishman in some other solitary room that the guest who had just departed was Lord Beeron's living image.

❧Molto bene. *But for those who are bored by carbohydrates, no matter how many wonderful ways they're served, there is always shopping. Leather, jewelry, high fashion, tight leather pants, high fashion jewelry, high-tech doo-dads, folky doo-dads, it's all there for the asking. The small joys and the great idiocies of shopping in Italy are discussed below by the queen of travel humorists Emily Kimbrough and by P. G. Konody, a humorous travel writer who has been all but forgotten.*

Emily Kimbrough
I Love Bargaining 1954

I CAME TO A SHOP just off St. Mark's Square that displayed in its window Olivetti portable typewriters. At home I had heard of these typewriters, how light they were to carry, how easy to handle. I had had in mind the purchase of one in Rome. It startled me to see them here. Venice seemed such a strange environment for a typewriter. Had I thought of the Venice world of affairs, I would have pictured its business conducted in a fine Italian hand.

I went inside and was greeted by a beautiful young woman behind the counter. I asked if she spoke English, and she said apologetically it was not very good. If such a beauty, I thought, were in New York I doubted she would be selling typewriters for very long; her photograph modeling the most expensive clothes would be in every fashion magazine. She had lifted a typewriter to the top of a counter, removed it from its case and was explaining rapidly to me in charming English all its technical virtues. Since I know only enough about a typewriter to punch its keys, and even then only when I look, I gave her discourse little attention.

But when she had finished I said it sounded just what I wanted, and that I would purchase it. A look of dismay clouded her exquisite features. Surely I would not make the purchase now, she protested, I asked if some special permit were required. She did not understand this at first, but when she had grasped my question denied vigorously such a necessity. She must speak to the owner, she explained, to secure permission for a little adjustment in price to be made.

I am not so untraveled as to be ignorant of the bargaining that accompanies purchases abroad, but somehow I had supposed such maneuvering was for incidentals like dresses and pocketbooks. Mechanical things, I had assumed, would be on an inflexibly realistic basis. I was delighted to find this was not so. I love bargaining. I would come back, I promised, next day.

As I turned to go another young woman came through from the back of the shop. She carried a baby on her arm, was the sister of my saleslady, and we were introduced; the baby was her six months old son. We chatted a few minutes, I played with the baby, who was adorable, learned a good deal of his sleeping and eating habits. They all three saw me on my way, the young man's arm propelled by his mother to a good-by wave. * * *

In the afternoon we hired a gondola and were photographed in it, giggling appropriately while this was done. Any tourist who feeds the pigeons in St. Mark's does not leave undone the other things that tourists should do. We stopped at the Ca'd'Oro, and when we found a crowd there and joined it to gape at an English motion picture company filming *Romeo and Juliet*, felt we were really in the tourist pattern.

Back at the hotel later in the afternoon I left my companions and went off on another solitary exploration. A particular delight in Venice, I think, is to take walks. In the first place, because at the onset it seems impossible with canals everywhere, and in the second place, because getting lost is inevitable and very pleasant. The streets are no wider than our sidewalks. They curve and turn bewilderingly. At the moment you are sure you are about to step back into St. Mark's, which is the sun from which all byways radiate, you find you have turned instead into a street you had not seen before. And contrariwise, at the very instant you feel totally lost you round a bend and are back at St. Mark's.

About five o'clock I rounded a bend and found myself outside the typewriter shop. I went in, had delightful conversation with my friends of the day before, including the baby, and learned the price of the typewriter had been reduced especially for me by two dollars. I assured my saleslady and her sister my gratitude and asked it to be relayed to the proprietor, adding that I would take the machine along. My friends were appalled. The sisters simultaneously exclaimed, surely I could come back the following day. They could now assure my definite interest in the machine and something more undoubtedly could be accomplished. I told them I was leaving the following day and could give only one more visit to this transaction. They were downcast at this news regretting that I was allotting such a brief time to this undertaking, but promised to achieve as much as was possible with only another twenty-four hours in which to work. And again I was waved off from the threshold. * * *

The following was our last day in Venice. In the morning Sophy and Zella went to see the Lido, by boat of course. I stayed behind because I had more important things to do. Mission typewriter was to be accomplished at half-past ten. But first I went to the address on my receipt to collect the finished prints of the photographs that had been taken of us the day before in the gondola. The photographer's studio was perhaps two minutes' walk from St. Mark's Square and I reached it in a little over half an hour. The streets I walked and that turned out to be not the ones indicated on my receipt, were charming and totally unfamiliar, though I thought I had covered that entire area on previous promenades. It made a pleasant excursion.

A good many other tourists were waiting for their photographs when I finally arrived at the proper place. The last obstacle had been three very steep flights of stairs. I was wheezing audibly when I crossed the threshold; so, I noticed immediately, were some of the others, evidently recent arrivals. We smiled at one another understandingly and one customer rose from the only chair in the room, offering it to me.

There were certainly ten of us in a space not much bigger than the average bathroom at home. Conversation was in French and German. Another customer wheezed in and I relinquished my chair. It was a kind of "Going to Jerusalem" in reverse. No one in the group seemed to belong to the establishment, but presently a young man bustled between bead portieres across a doorway, carrying a considerable pile of envelopes. He was at the far end of the room.

He pushed his way through us to a table in a corner. He put his pile of envelopes down on it, patted them and looked inquiringly from one to the other of us. We handed him our respective receipts, those of us the farthest away passing them on from neighbor to neighbor. The young man sorted through his pile, found the envelope that matched the receipt number and delivered it. Immediately he received it, each customer opened his and took out the photographs. Everyone was interested so there was a general distribution and it took a little time to reassemble the sets. Payment was somewhat involved, too, due to lack of space and the fact that the young photographer had no change. But in the group we made change for one another.

Later in the day when I showed the photographs to Zella and Sophy, I found my set included a shot of a smiling stout German couple and recognized the woman as the one who had given me her chair.

I went on to the typewriter shop, and found waiting there the two sisters, the baby, the baby's grandmother and her son, the younger brother of the two girls. We were introduced immediately and shook hands all around, my financial intermediary acting as interpreter and explaining to me that Mama and Luigi had come to offer me felicitations on the purchase of the beautiful little machine and congratulations on the news I was about to receive. My saleslady paused dramatically. Everyone watched me, their eyes shining.

A further adjustment had been made, she announced, and smiled modestly at such achievement. Because of the friendship Italy felt for America and pride that an Italian machine was going to be taken to New York, from the price for which this machine was always sold, five dollars was to be removed. She flung out her arm and opened her hand wide. It was beautiful, as if we all saw the five dollars floating through the open door. No one could speak for a moment, then Mama gave a deep sigh— "Aaaah," she said.

I followed with, *"Grazie, grazie, grazie,"* and we shook hands all around, the baby's hand put by his mother into mine.

As I was counting out the money, Mama requested our interpreter to ask if I were a secretary to an American millionaire. I understood, however, and by putting *scribo* and *libro* together, and adding an inspiring pantomime of myself at a microphone, conveyed to these charming and astute people that I wrote books and talked on the radio. The ahs and sighs that followed this announcement could have blown that five dollars all the way to the farthest canal. I was requested to shake hands all around again, and I shook the hand of each, including the baby.

I thought I could make my exit on this, but I was mistaken. The typewriter I had been shown was not the one I was allowed to take. A fresh one was brought from the storeroom, unpacked from its outer carton, removed from its carrying case, turned on the counter toward me with the request that I try it to make sure the action suited me. If not, another would be brought out.

In some embarrassment from the unblinking attention of the family, I typed out, "Now is the time for all good men to come to the aid of the party," and pronounced the machine exactly to my liking.

Mama asked if I would be so gracious as to autograph the sentiment I had just expressed and allow her to keep it as a memento from an American writer. I have never before wittingly appropriated someone else's prose, but I left with Mama that sentence as my own creation, and I hope I may be forgiven for it. Daughter, I knew, was not going to have an easy time translating it for Mama. I hoped they would think of me as a writer of profound and abstruse philosphy.

The need to leave, I felt, was urgent and I expressed this. The news was greeted by little cries of regret, but understanding. The typewriter was snapped back into its carrying case, and I had got as far as the door when young brother opening it for me told us it was starting to rain. This announcement provoked a little drama and considerable delay. It was not to be considered, Mama declared, that I should go out into the rain. My clothes, my beautiful new machine; all, all would be ruined. I endeavored to explain the alternative of my missing the train to Milan, and Mama gave in on condition that her son, provided with an umbrella, would accompany me back to the hotel. The umbrella was produced from a back room. I shook hands all around once more, baby included, and the last I saw of the family as I set off was baby's arm propelled in a farewell salute.

P. G. Konody
I'll Have None of That 1911

W E ARE IN ITALY! was the first clear thought that flashed across the awakening consciousness next morning, engendered perhaps by the excessively brilliant light filtering through the chinks of the Venetian blinds. The restraining influence of the early hour and the enticing comfort of the typically Italian bed at the Scudo di Francia (where in the wide world are to be found hotel beds that can vie with those of Italy?) were insufficient to counteract the eagerness to be up and about. I dressed in haste, determined to steal a march on my companions, and to explore Ivrea before breakfast, since the day's long programme would necessitate a fairly early start. Ryder, indeed, was already busying himself about the car which, cleared of her thick layer of dust, had become recognisable once more. The duty of inspection absolved, I stepped out into the piazza—and almost ran into Pomponius, who, urged by an impulse similar to my own, had risen at an early hour and was just returning from his morning walk, beaming with the unreasoning joy experienced by every sensitive Northerner on his first contact with Southern life and sunlight.

But another cause had contributed to Pomponius's cheerfulness. With a courage vastly ahead of his extremely limited command of the Italian language, he had been marketing on his own. His booty was a large parcel of figs, and the double triumph of having achieved an extraordinary bargain and of being able to deliver a blow to my often reiterated faith in Italian honesty. Pomponius, ever concerned about his physical welfare, was a firm believer in the efficacy of fruit before breakfast. The tempting wares displayed in the market square had proved irresistible to him. According to his own account of his adventure, there were things that he had never seen before: vegetable or fruit—who could say? He was most attracted by the bright colour of the *peperoni;* but he preferred to be on the safe side of the known. He pointed at a basket with juicy figs, and drawing extensively upon his Italian vocabulary, boldly addressed the corpulent dame who presided over the stall: *"Fichi—quanto?"*

The answer was voluble and friendly, but to him wholly unintelligible. So he produced the equivalent of two English pennies, whereupon the kindly old soul smilingly proceeded upon picking out her juiciest specimens for her strange customer. "Now, where is your vaunted Italian honesty?" commented Pomponius, "the old wretch was going to give me all the rotten, perspiring, burst, sticky fruit. But I would have none of it. I said, 'no, no,' and had my own pick. I must admit, she wasn't stingy. When I had enough she still insisted on filling the bag. Look at the beauties—all the lot for four soldi!" And he proudly displayed his purchase of carefully selected, hard, unripe figs.

Shopping for a hotel room is not quite as much fun as shopping for gifts for yourself and for those who expect something back home. If you're the type who likes the challenge of finding new accommodations every other day or so, you've probably wondered why, even two hundred miles from the nearest museum or cathedral, there never seems to be a vacancy. If instead, you're the type who books everything in advance, only to find that a week in Venice is six days too many or too few, even you may find yourself doing some shopping around. Well, the Hungaro-British king of travel humor, George Mikes, has solved the Italian hotel puzzle with all the genius of his fellow-countryman Rubik.

George Mikes
No Vacancies 1956

WHY ARE ITALIAN HOTELS FULL all the time? Because of the engineers' conferences.

We could not get a room in Verona because—we were told—the engineers were having a conference in the town. We could not get a room in Padua because the same engineers—or perhaps other engineers—were having another conference there, too. A few weeks later I could not get a room in Trieste. "There is not a single room to be had in the whole town," a hotel-porter told me. "The best thing you can do is to drive to Udine or Monfalcone and try there. Even there you may find it difficult." He added in explanation: "You see, the engineers are having a conference in the town."

In no travel guide is this basic fact mentioned that engineers are having a conference in all Italian towns all the time.

I saw many of these engineers—I could not help seeing them. We usually met at breakfast time. Every hotel restaurant was teeming between 8 and 9:30 A.M. with gay and lively engineers—ready for breakfast and eager to confer afterwards. They all wore a red or blue label of some kind in their buttonholes. They brought curious objects out of enormous brief-cases. The object—more often than not—consisted of a metal rod with a ring in the middle, in which there was a box-like instrument which could be rotated round the rod. At the end of the rod there was something they could pull out and push in again. The object seemed rather dull and childish to the lay eye but it was a source of endless delight, fascination and awe to all engineers.

And what—I asked myself—if one cannot get a room in Italian hotels? It is indeed a small price to pay for the happiness of the engineers.

Of course, you may always have a room reserved in advance: and if you receive a confirmation from an Italian hotel stating that a room has, in fact, been reserved for you, that may mean many things. It does not even entirely exclude the possibility that a room has been reserved for you. But it would be almost enchanting naïveté to count on it.

In Rome, for example, they accept twenty per cent more reservations than the number of people they can accommodate. People who have rooms reserved often do not turn up; but then again they often do and that's just too bad for them. In the season hundreds of people are turned away from hotels in Rome—people who booked and were accepted. Many people are driven to the conclusion that it is simpler to be turned away from hotels without previous reservation.

In any Italian city after five or six in the afternoon you may see people in cars—foreign and provincial cars—slowly and sadly cruising the town. The car is overloaded with luggage; the husband is driving; his wife is anxiously scrutinising a clumsily folded map and directing her husband—usually in the wrong direction. This overcrowding of hotels and consequent desperate search for rooms, I was told, is extremely beneficial economically:

(1) the cruising motorists use up petrol thus helping the oil companies;

(2) they frequently stop for refeshments, thus helping the catering industry;

(3) they ensure that all the hotels are full all the time—and that is why hotel-keepers resist all attempts to build more hotels.

And what—I asked myself again—if one cannot get a room in any hotel in Italy? Is it not indeed a small price to pay for the happiness of oil companies, caterers and hotel-keepers?

Yet, however often one is told that it is impossible to get a room in an Italian hotel as all the hotels are always full, there seems to be a flaw in this reasoning. Hotels must be full of people who actually did succeed in getting rooms. Indeed, I should go as far as to say, that the fuller the hotels are, the more people managed to get in.

When you think of love in Italy, you never think of hotel rooms (that's love back home). Rather, you think of the countryside, strolling across a meadow; or the northern lakes, sitting together by the shore listening to the water and staring up at the mountains; or the Riviera, sunbathing together with almost nothing on. But most of all, especially if you're a woman, you recall the city streets, being followed, stalked, chased, and pinched; you remember the most suave, handsome gentlemen suddenly turning into savage animals. Is this stereotype a false one? Has the Italian man, tight pants and all, been wrongfully maligned? And has the Italian woman, too, been falsely portrayed by the Sophia Lorens and Gina Lollabrigidas of the world? Will the fantasies of the poor, innocent, passionless English-speaking tourist be dissolved into the thinnest of airs? Below, three experts on the phenomenon of love in Italy will shed light on the Italian man: for the male tourist's viewpoint, Art Buchwald; for the female tourist, Edith Templeton; and with a fine little tale that says more than a thousand paintings, Anthony Thorne.

Art Buchwald
American in Rome 1962

THE BIG MISTAKE WAS TAKING MY WIFE to Rome in the first place. Any American husband in his right mind should know better than to bring his spouse to Italy, particularly for the first time. But I underestimated the Italians, which is kind of hard to do.

It all started when my wife came back to the Excelsior Hotel from a shopping trip to the Via Condotti. She had a big grin on her face.

"What's so funny?" I wanted to know.

"Three Italians flirted with me on the street today," she said, pleased with herself.

"Well, don't let it go to your head," I warned her. "They flirt with everybody."

"Don't be too sure," she said. "Besides, the Roman men make you feel like you're really a woman."

"I make you feel like you're a woman, too," I said angrily.

"Did you every call me Blue Eyes?" she wanted to know.

"No, and for a very simple reason. You don't have blue eyes."

"That's not the point. Even if they lie, they do it beautifully. I think Italian men are wonderful."

I decided to drop the subject before I really lost my temper. But the next day, after another shopping tour, there she stood with the same smile on her face.

"Okay," I said, "what happened today?"

"A traffic policeman stopped all the traffic on the Via Veneto so I could cross the street."

"Big deal," I said. "It so happens that traffic policemen are supposed to stop traffic so people can cross the street. That's their job."

"When the light is green?" she asked. "Then, as I crossed, he tipped his hat and all the cars were blowing their horns. It's never happened to me in any other city."

"Of course it hasn't. In most cities traffic cops are trying to save people's lives," I said. "So he tipped his hat. He was just looking for an opportunity to take it off. Those helmets can get very hot, you know."

"Don't be so smart," she said. "If you want further proof that Italian men really care, this morning I ordered a coffee at Doney's and the waiter couldn't have been nicer."

"So what? Some waiters are nice. What does that prove?"

"Nothing, except *he* picked up the check."

She was getting impossible and the next afternoon I was afraid to come back to the room.

The smile was waiting for me.

"I know," I said. "You went to Bulgari's and the salesman gave you a diamond necklace as a free souvenir from Rome."

"Nothing that dramatic," she said. "But a taxi driver asked me to go dancing with him tonight."

"Wait a minute. You don't speak Italian. How do you know he asked you to go dancing tonight."

"He held up his hands as if he was holding somebody in them and he hummed a waltz."

"What's so great about that?"

"The cab was moving while he did it."

There was nothing I could say to that, so I tried to walk out of the room.

"I think you're absolutely terrible," she said. "Everyone has been so nice and all you want to do is to throw cold water on me. You American men just don't know how to appreciate a woman."

"Is that so," I said. "Well, it so happens I have a cousin who went up to a girl on Fifth Avenue in New York and told her she had the most beautiful figure he had ever seen, and he's now doing twenty years in Sing Sing. Ever since then I've kept my thoughts to myself."

Edith Templeton
Highly Prized c1957

HERE I MUST TOUCH UPON A POINT of travel in Italy which has not been mentioned by any of the famous travellers, like Goethe, Heine, Smollett, and Lord Byron in past centuries, or by D. H. Lawrence or Aldous Huxley in the present. They could not mention it because they did not know it, and they did not know it because they were men. The point is: What is it like for a foreign woman to travel through Italy?

I think I am very well suited to make a few observations on this subject because I am a woman, and neither young nor beautiful. Therefore my experiences are, so to speak, reduced to the lowest common denominator. If I had the face of a Garbo and the charm of a Marlene Dietrich I would never presume to generalize.

The foreign woman, be she fifteen or fifty, is highly prized as an acquisition by the Italian man. Often she is approached in the most harmless and impeccable manner but, whatever the opening, it is merely a short prelude. Very soon the Italian gets to the core of what is in his mind with a directness which some women find funny, some childish, some insulting, some disarmingly sincere, some flattering, some disgusting.

Furthermore, it is not only the speed and the directness of his approach, but also his perseverance, which the foreign woman finds astonishing.

It is quite a usual occurrence in, say, Florence and Venice, where the native men are specially foreigner-minded, that a man will follow a woman traveller through the streets for literally hours. Or, if he has found out where she lives, he will hang about in front of the house for literally days, hoping to find an occasion for catching sight of her and speaking to her. The traveller's hair will probably be wispy, her grey flannel skirt will be creased, and her blouse crumpled from frequent packing and unpacking. She will wear ugly and comfortable shoes because she has to walk miles a day through the heat, from one palace to another, and she will be aware of her dowdiness, as she observes the many young, pretty, well-groomed and well-dressed Italian women who move through the same town as the foreigner and who yet are never being followed in the streets, are never pestered when they visit museums, are never chased when they sit down on a bench in a park.

The Italian seems to be blind to these ravishing creatures, and the foreign woman is to him what the sun is to the sunflower. To her the Italian scene is peopled with men who try to make assignations. Even the policeman whom she has asked the way to Santa Croce regrets that as he is on duty he cannot accompany her now—but what about meeting in the evening? During my first stay in Italy I had experiences like these, and kept saying to myself: "This happens to me. But it does not happen to an Italian woman. Why? What is the matter with me? What have I done to make these men behave in such a forward manner?" and the whole time I felt I was playing a game of which I did not know the rules. "I travel alone. I like talking to people. Why am I not able to talk to Italians without giving them the idea that I am a tart who has reduced her fees?"

It took me several years to find the explanation, and what I offer here may not be the whole truth, but certainly is a great deal of it: The Italian behaviour springs from two main streams: calculation and vanity.

His common sense tells him that he cannot go wrong if he has an affair with a foreigner travelling by herself. If she is married, there is no husband on the spot who could be awkward. If she is a young girl, she cannot make him marry her because she has not got the hold over him which an Italian woman has. She cannot set her whole family to his heels and threaten to blacken his name in the whole town. She cannot make trouble for him if there should be any consequences to the affair because she would find it impossible to sue him for paternity across a thousand miles.

In other words, he can behave as irresponsibly as he wants to and he knows that no punishment will befall him.

With his own countrywomen, things are different. Hardly has he been seen promenading on the Corso with a young girl, than Mama will already want to know what his intentions are. And if, by a lucky chance, Mama does not get on to his scent, the girl herself will put in some good work and dissolve into tears and throw scenes in order to make him declare himself, and he will have to fight for every kiss. But most often he will not even get as far as this. Much as she might like to, a young Italian girl cannot afford to have a lover. Towns are small and life is narrow, and once she is known to have slipped, her chances of ever getting married are poor. No wonder that the realistic Italian thinks that a foreigner in the hand is better than two lovely Italian girls in the bush.

Add to this the fact that the young Italian has been brought up on brothels and is, therefore, not choosy. He is as sensitive to beauty in woman as any other man, but owing to his amatory upbringing he has learnt to compromise.

Now we come to the other mainspring, governed by vanity. This is maintained by a long tradition. For centuries Italy has been the education and playground of the young northerner of good family, English, German, and Scandinavian. This gave birth to the very understandable belief among Italians that every Englishman was a 'Milord', and monstrously rich into the bargain. A tradition like this does not die easily. Even to-day, when travel abroad is no longer a privilege of the ruling class, the Italian has not yet weaned himself of this prejudice. Also, since America has become a world Power there has been a steady industry of providing husbands of noble Italian birth for American heiresses. Considering all this is so natural, that to the average Italian it is a matter of prestige to hook a foreign woman, no matter for how short a time. It is a conquest to be shown off on the Corso, to be bragged about in the café, to be boasted of not only to friends but to acquaintances.

But, you will say, surely it takes two to make a love affair. Of course it does.

Consider the ordinary English or German girl. Quite pretty, quite pleasant, but not very striking. In her own country she has had to work hard to find admirers. Her escorts to dances and parties did not grow on trees. In a discreet way she has had to chase the men and she has never been chased herself. Now she comes to Italy. She is told she is beautiful and men swoon at her sight. She is told that her charms make a man's blood run hot. She is showered with attentions such as she never knew before, and I must admit that, when an Italian wants to be attentive and devoted, he is much better at it than other men. To him this is all routine; but the young girl does not stop to think that, if he had not made the same identical protestations of love a hundred times before, he would not be so good at it.

And so, even if her admirer does not particularly appeal to her, her head will be turned and she will be an easy conquest.

Or take the other extreme: the wealthy woman of about fifty who has been a good wife and mother for the last thirty years, who finds herself widowed and wants to see the world. After having lived for so long with a bore she will fall even more easily than the young woman. Contrary to common belief, it is not the young who yearn for romance; it is the middle-aged.

And the harder she is on the surface, the softer she will be in her heart. The grimly efficient career woman who has looked after a business with all the ruses of a masculine brain, and who could see through a confidence-trickster in half a minute, will lose herself to the Italian who is nothing more than an amorous confidence-man. His job is easy. The well-worn clichés work well when nature does his wooing for him, with silky air, moonlight on ruins, and the lapping of waves against a distant shore.

The disintegration is quick. I remember once, in Taormina, a Swedish countess of about fifty who was cashing a cheque in front of me at the bank. She was got up like a widow of Royalty in ankle-length black draperies, and with a widow's cap with a heart-shaped peak pointing down the forehead, and a black veil. She was chatting with the cashier, and from her talk I gathered that she had just arrived in Taormina and intended to look for a house, to settle down in modest retirement.

I returned to Taormina half a year later. Like so many of her kind before her, she had become one of the sights of the village. Not only had she shed her weeds but she had been forced to take a short trip to Sweden in order to sell some securities because her Taorminese lover cost her very dear. So exuberant had she become that she used to enter shops, stop on the threshold, throw herself into a mock operatic attitude, and sing as though she were on the stage: "Be greeted, good people. My husband is dead."

My advice to the woman tourist who is pestered in the street by an Italian is: do not try to ignore him. If you do he may follow you for hours and spoil the whole afternoon for you. When he comes out with his usual request to be allowed to accompany you, say something like: "Alas, it is not possible."

"But why is it not possible?"

"Because I am on my way to meet my lover."

"Perhaps I am better than your lover. Is he nice?"

Put a hand on your heart, turn your eyes heavenward and say: "He is—I can't tell you how wonderful."

This will get rid of him. I guarantee the success.

In cases like these, Italians are like children. It is not enough to say no. "How no?" they will say. They must know why it is no. And they will go to great lengths to sway you.

Once in Naples I was pursued by one of the porters in my hotel. At first I said: "It's no use, you know. You will not get any money out of me."

"Ah, but I am not thinking of money."

"Sweet of you," I said, "but even so, forget about it."

"I am even prepared to spend money on you, madam. If it embarrasses you to see me in this hotel I will take a room in another hotel. Will you let me?"

"No," I said.

He made his last bid. "Look here, madam. I am a very good lover. Please try me. As you know, I am employed in this hotel. If you are not satisfied with me you can complain to the *padrone* about me and he will give me the sack."

If you are a stay-at-home do not be impressed by your friend who returns from Italy full of "adventures". My mother had a word for it. She would say: "What do you mean by 'adventures'? She just does not know how to say 'no'".

Anthony Thorne
Beautifully Done 1957

THE BEACH TOO HAS ITS SURPRISES—its familiar pattern of basking, swimming, sailing and exploring is shattered one day by a phenomenon so extraordinary that the whole island will be talking of it.

First of all, down a flight of steps that lead from the beach-door of the restaurant there walks a girl in a black satin bathing dress and with a white straw hat set jauntily on a head of soap-sud ash-blonde curls. The effect could easily have been that of a film magazine, but her extreme youth and naturalness turn blatancy into mere impertinence. She herself, with her shell-like fairness of skin and hair, is a wild surprise—some Norwegian yacht must at last have discovered Procida. But then, a moment later, with the same beautifully slow movements, there descends a second young girl, *indistinguishable from the first*. They link arms together, beauty with its image, and walk coolly and delicately along the beach.

They are, of course, identical twins parading their incredible similarity, and it was unfair of Nature to have said the same thing twice. The effect on the place as they pass, apparently indifferent to the sensation they are making, is no less than volcanic. All eyes follow them with awe, gymnastics cease, a canoe capsizes, a beach-ball drifts unheeded in the direction of Africa, mouths gape, an umbrella breaks off at its stem, and two young Italians, unable to bear the spectacle a moment longer, are forced to fling themselves into the jungle of canes behind Chiaiolella.

One beautiful blond girl, yes, and how welcome in this context—but *two* of them, and identical, are an embarrassment. The eye is confused, and so are the mind and the body. Is this a vision of Helen appearing in duplicate to a rather drunken Doctor Faustus?

The twins are obviously inseparable, and their sensitive physical and mental relationship to one another is apparent even at a distance. As though in a mirror, the turning of one head is immediately reflected by the turning of the other. They must have some private radar, of which those who are not identical twins can know nothing.

Confusion spreads as they walk, and I see now that our brilliant jack-knife diver, having climbed to the peak of his rock, is complacently looking round for his appreciative audience. Are we watching him? Not this time, my lad—and it appears that even he is being hypnotized by the girls as they approach him. If only I had a pair of binoculars I would study his expression. What can be happening up there?

Steady, now, think what you are doing! He tenses, relaxes, tenses again, pauses, has second thoughts, drops his arms, gives one more startled glance over his shoulder, lurches, slips, and with a wild cry—echoed by all of us—hurls himself into space.

The splash is tremendous. We hold our breaths, for diving untidily from such a height he could easily have broken his neck. But a few moments later, dripping with salt water and mortification, he hauls himself clumsily out of the sea. Fortunately for him the duplicate Helens, ending one half of their morning's stroll in sweet ignorance of the uproar they have caused, have already turned their backs on him—simultaneously....

And tonight is my last night on Procida. I had meant to stay no more than three days in this 'port of call', but even my watch has stopped and the calendar in my diary has become a convenient blur. I must either go or stay here for ever, and common sense has fixed my departure for tomorrow morning. For tonight I had already made plans, but I revise them hastily. Nothing must keep me from that absurdly over-romantic dance floor. In the dusky light of the stars and of Ischia and of the lamps of distant octopus-fishers, in the scent of jasmine, and to the sentimental throbs of Neapolitan music, something interesting should surely happen. Come what may, I must watch the effect of these extraordinary young women on the swarthy Casanovas of the beach.

So much one could have guessed. Here, just as soon as the music begins, and while diners are still peeling their last peaches, arrives the entire male population of the place, with silkier ties and glossier hair and teeth more glittering than they have ever been before. When will those twins arrive? For an hour or more the lads dance off-handedly with the Italian girls, their too expressive eyes flashing incessantly at the entrance.

At long last, wearing pale moth-coloured dresses that with their pallor of skin and hair give them the effect of beautiful manifestations at a séance, these girls arrive—chaperoned by an elderly man who looks like a distinguished Norwegian diplomat. They sit down and order champagne, apparently unconscious that the Italians are devouring them by inches.

What will happen? How will these men ever conquer the atmosphere of inaccessibility with which twins always seem to be surrounded? I must miss nothing. Every moment must be recorded. I have produced my notebook and a pen. To my annoyance a small boy, arriving from nowhere, is plucking at my sleeve.

"Don Aurelio's compliments," he says, "and will you eat grapes with him tomorrow evening at seven?"

It is a peculiarly pleasant invitation—"grapes at seven". I am used to the less conventional appointments and am delighted to be asked to breakfast with American friends, but to grapes at seven I have never yet been bidden. It even rings of the ancient world, when in the peace of a glowing sunset one might walk among the vines of a companion, eating random bunches and discussing by turns trivialities and matters of importance... But tomorrow I shall be gone, and so I must scribble a hasty *biglietto* for the boy to take back to his master. I conclude it by saying: "The thanks that I really owe to you shall be given to your Procida, as I know you will wish."

Then, after a moment of regret for my departure—the reasons for leaving a place that has captured one are always so unbearably simple—I raise my eyes eagerly to the dance floor, to see what is happening.

Nothing is happening—nothing whatever. There is music still, but nobody is dancing. Ludicrously, the restaurant cat strolls across the floor. Otherwise, the place is paralysed. The luminously pale Norwegian girls are talking quietly and happily with their father, unaware that arrows and darts of love are falling silently around them. Am I to believe that these bold, resourceful and energetic Italian males are completely defeated by the sight of twins—by two coins of female beauty that happen to have been cast in the same mould? What inhibits them? Surely the courtesy of asking the father's permission would present no difficulty to these civilized creatures?

But—yes, I begin to imagine it myself—*which* girl does one ask to dance, and if that one, why not the other (to dance with both being impossible), and in the second dance (when one would of course hold her a little closer) might she not, by some mistake, be her sister? All sorts of unimaginable confusions and complexities are threatening—they could even lead to a serious breach between sworn friends, and to undying family feuds. The plot, already thick, has obstinately congealed, and we are all aware of it. But what is to happen?

Our music has expired now, for lack of encouragement. There is a stupid pause. And then, for the Italians may be defeated in war but in nothing in civilized living, there comes the answer. Suddenly, with a precision equalling that of the twins' instinctively correlated movements, all these young men throw back their heads, open their mouths, and sing.

They sing. They make love to both these girls simultaneously with their fine voices, since they find difficulty in touching them with their hands; they pour out their admiration and their desire in all the songs that they can remember. There is lush Neapolitan sentimentality, of course—one could not expect otherwise—but there is also a passion expressed in tones so subtle and haunting that they seem to have come from Africa. And there are gay songs too—so gay, indeed, that at times I cannot help hoping that these young Norwegians do not understand the words too well... Each touches her cheek at the same moment, with the same gesture, and from the glow in their faces it is evident that at least they understand and appreciate the music, which has been aimed not only at their bodies but at their hearts.

The father, I think, realizes the complexities of the situation, and at a moment when thirsty throats are calling for the waiter he skilfully intercepts him and contrives, piloting his daughters slowly across the floor and out of the restaurant, to leave every man a glass in which to drink their health.

It has been beautifully done. The girls have gone and nobody attempts to follow them. There is a vast communal sigh. And then throats refreshed begin singing again as though they were still there, or as though they had dematerialized but would certainly appear again. And I realize that I am still holding my pen, and that up to now I have written nothing.

A TOUR TO BOOT

⭐Getting Around

⭐*Although many of us are happy just to be able to hit two of the Big Three, others like to get away from the beaten tracks that all lead to Rome and to see the countryside, the mountains, the coasts, the islands, and the secondary (for tourist purposes) cities. Italy is much larger and more varied a place than most people think. It has nearly every climate but equatorial, nearly every height, from the tallest point in Europe to sea level—and there's lots of that— and nearly every level of density, from the remotest mountain village to the residential districts of Naples.*

Everyone knows the country is shaped like a boot, but what few people know is what style the boot is. Well, it's clearly a Western boot, considering which American states fit snugly into its total area: Arizona, Colorado, Nevada, and Wyoming; and New Mexico could probably wedge itself in. Internationally, the size fits not quite all: Ecuador, Gabon, New Zealand, Oman, and, of course, the Phillippines—at least when Imelda Marcos was still around. Poland would have to borrow a heavy shoe-horn from its neighborly brother, and the U.K. would have to settle for one size too big. Yes sir, Italy is a really big shoe.

So how do you get around it? Well, chariots are no longer in fashion, so that leaves the usual: trains, buses, automobiles, and the national form of transportation, the Vespa. Trains are relaxing and chummy, depending on how many barnyard animals your neighbors bring. Buses are bumpy and even more chummy, depending on how

much garlic your neighbors have eaten and how super-
stitious they are about opening windows. Cars aren't the
least bit relaxing or chummy, unless you hook up with
someone around a tight curve; then suddenly you will
have no problem at all finding someone to speak Italian
with you, and he'll speak it clearly and loud, repeating
certain unfamiliar words, particularly about family mat-
ters, over and over again, so that you can learn them by
heart. Vespas are probably best left to the natives; in
keeping with their name, which translates as "wasp" or
"hornet," they can be a hornet's nest of trouble. Or, for
the right person, a lot of fun.

Italian trains may not run on time anymore, but they
make up for every late second with entertainment. Our
own train entertainment includes Irish novelist Sean
O'Faolain on the joys of trying to switch your ticket;
British travel writer H. V. Morton on the sort of tourists
one can expect to share one's compartment with; Charles
Dickens on what trains are best for: reverie; and, last but
certainly not least, D. H. Lawrence on the romance of the
Italian countryside as seen from the window of a train.

Sean O'Faolain
Pazienza! 1953

HOW TURBULENT THE ROMAN CROWDS seem
after the steady quiet rumbling beside the blue sea
and the red earth, and the somnolent isolation of my
compartment! But there is George waiting for me with
his car, and the Roman ban on motor-horns gives some
quiet to the Sunday evening streets; and George and
Carlotta live on a quiet corner of Monte Sacro on the
eastern edge of the city, with one arched window of their
flat facing south and one facing east, so that as we dine
we see a noble line of umbrella pines against the mountains, and the Alban Hills, and Rocca di Papa, and the

motionless baby clouds, and we look out over Tivoli and Castelli.

I romance about the peace of Italy and George gets furious, and says:

"You try to get a *permesso di soggiorno!* You try to import a radio! A friend in America has been writing that she is sending us a lunch-basket. We have been writing back to her saying, 'Please, please, *please* do not send us a lunch-basket!'" Now the lunch-basket has arrived. "Six times," wails George, with his fists to the ceiling, "six times I have been down to that blasted office…"

I spent the better part of the whole of the next day trying to switch the route of my tickets at the railway station. Upstairs, downstairs, here, there, *scusa, per favore,* fill this form, fill that form, *prego,* going to the wrong office, *per niente,* and then being sent to the right office, *scusa,* and finding it was the wrong office, *che peccato,* and that the wrong office had been the right office, *grazie, scusa, scusa, per favore…Per Dio!* This Italian pen! But it is in every sense fatal to put pen to paper in Italy. If you have a piece of paper it means that three or four officials will argue over it; and on the other hand, if you have not a piece of paper the three or four officials come to tell you that you must get a piece of paper for them to argue over it. As I sat, angry and exhausted, in the last office of all, I thought, looking at the man who was supposed to be dealing with me, "He can look out every day at the ruins of the baths of Diocletian, and the sky-signs, CIM, *Grandi Magazini,* PERUGINA, *Cioccolata Caramella,* MARTINI, and the plume and curve of the fountain in the Piazza Ezedra, and the Grand Hotel, and the never-stirring clouds above the Tiber and the Janiculum, and, alas, that is all I know, or ever will know about him because I am too tired, too cross and too shy to ask him to come out for a drink, and, anyway, blast him, I don't want to hear his life-story. *I want my tickets!*" Scratch, scratch! What on earth can he be writing?

"Excuse me! I must go to another office."

Pazienza! Eternally, *pazienza!* Is this why they are so excitable? Patience so prolonged must make any human being's nerves go like Madhouse Ward Number 999.

I barely caught my evening train to Naples.

H. V. Morton
A Jolly Canadian Couple 1964

THE TRAIN IN WHICH I WAS TRAVELLING is the most elegant in Europe, probably, I should say, in the world. It has a name and a voice. The name, *Settebello*— the "beautiful seven"—is that of an Italian card game in which the winning card is the Seven of Diamonds; and the accomplished voice of the train, speaking perfectly in English, French, and German, as well as in its native Italian, described to us the seven beautiful air-conditioned coaches which link Rome so pleasantly with Milan. The voice had the air of an Italian nobleman casually showing off the treasures of his palace to a guest. Listening to it, as it gently issued from concealed loud-speakers, and glancing round the cool drawing-room in which I sat, where all the luggage, and even the squalid parcels which one accumulates in Italy, were hidden behind panelling, I thought this was surely the most aristocratic form of movement since the coaches of the nobility rolled round Italy in the days of the Grand Tour. Indeed, I thought, had electric locomotives been invented during the Renaissance, this was just the kind of train that Ludovico Sforza and Beatrice d'Este would have owned, the restaurant car painted by Leonardo da Vinci.

My companions until Florence, where they left the train, were a jolly Canadian couple who told me they were paying their first visit to Europe. When I asked what had impressed them most in Rome, they replied the ghosts. I agreed, thinking that this was their way of describing the crowded events and characters of history; but no, they meant, literally, ghosts, spirits, phantoms. Their hotel in the middle of Rome had been haunted, and they had found the Colosseum as full of spirits as Cellini did when he spent a night there with a sorcerer. They did not actually complain of the spirits but mentioned them with amused tolerance, rather as good-natured travellers might refer to a lack of hot water or some other minor irritation. At the same time they gave the impression that they had stood no nonsense from them: they had kept the shades of Caesar and Borgia in their places. I can accept pale, nervous spiritualists who appear aware of the awful mysteries with which they are concerned, but jolly disciples of the occult who introduce a note of Rotarianism into their transactions with the other world are, to me, as frightening as a ghost itself. I waved to them at Florence and saw them vanish among porters and luggage (and goodness knows what else invisible to me), wondering which of the Medici they were about to buttonhole.

Charles Dickens
An Italian Dream 1844

I HAD BEEN TRAVELLING for some days; resting very little in the night, and never in the day. The rapid and unbroken succession of novelties that had passed before me came back like half-formed dreams; and a crowd of objects wandered in the greatest confusion through my mind, as I travelled on, by a solitary road. At intervals, some one among them would stop, as it were, in its restless flitting to and fro, and enable me to look at it, quite steadily, and behold it in full distinctness. After a few moments, it would dissolve, like a view in a magic-lantern; and while I saw some part of it quite plainly, and some faintly, and some not at all, would show me another of the many places I had lately seen, lingering behind it, and coming through it. This was no sooner visible than, in its turn, it melted into something else.

At one moment, I was standing again, before the brown old rugged churches of Modena. As I recognised the curious pillars with grim monsters for their bases, I seemed to see them, standing by themselves in the quiet square at Padua, where there were the staid old University, and the figures, demurely gowned, grouped here and there in the open space about it. Then I was strolling in the outskirts of that pleasant city, admiring the unusual neatness of the dwelling-houses, gardens, and orchards, as I had seen them a few hours before. In their stead arose, immediately, the two towers of Bologna; and the most obstinate of all these objects failed to hold its ground a minute before the monstrous moated castle of Ferrara, which, like an illustration to a wild romance, came back again in the red sunrise, lording it over the solitary, grass-grown, withered town. In short, I had that incoherent but delightful jumble in my brain, which travellers are apt to have, and are indolently willing to encourage. Every shake of the coach in which I sat, half dozing in the dark, appeared to jerk some new recollection out of its place, and to jerk some other new recollection into it; and in this state I fell asleep.

D. H. Lawrence
Lemon Trees 1921

IT IS ONLY THIRTY MILES TO MESSINA, but the train takes two hours. It winds and hurries and stops beside the lavender grey morning sea. A flock of goats trails over the beach near the lapping wave's edge, dismally. Great wide deserts of stony river-beds run down to the sea, and men on asses are picking their way across, and women are kneeling by the small stream-channel washing clothes. The lemons hang pale and innumerable in the thick lemon groves. Lemon trees, like Italians, seem to be happiest when they are touching one another all round. Solid forests of not very tall lemon trees lie between the steep mountains and the sea, on the strip of plain. Women, vague in the orchard under-shadow, are picking the lemons, lurking as if in the undersea. There are heaps of pale yellow lemons under the trees. They look like pale, primrose-smouldering fires. Curious how like fires the heaps of lemons look, under the shadow of foliage, seeming to give off a pallid burning amid the suave, naked, greenish trunks. When there comes a cluster of orange trees, the oranges are red like coals among the darker leaves. But lemons, lemons, innumerable, speckled like innumerable tiny stars in the green firmament of leaves. So many lemons! Think of all the lemonade crystals they will be reduced to! Think of America drinking them up next summer.

If romance is what you want out of Italy, you'd probably do well not to rent an automobile. Then again, if adventure is what you want, and you couldn't afford the Himalayas again this year, then don't pass up the chance to drive on an Italian autostrada. *And if you want to get to know Italians through and through, what makes them tick and then go off with a bang, nothing can provide you with more information than getting behind the wheel of a Fiat or an Alfa yourself.*

Although we don't have sufficient space here to provide you with a driver-training course for Italian roads, and since we know you don't really want to look at pages of road signs you'll never even see at 150 kph, we will at least prepare you for the inevitable, or cause you to choose the train. Listen carefully to travel humorist extraordinaire Art Buchwald.

Art Buchwald
Mafia Members Are Boy Scouts 1959

PALERMO—As a distinguished student of European driving habits and their effect on the human heart, I wish to make a statement. Of all the peoples I have studied so far, there are none to compare with the Sicilian drivers. One only has to be a few hours on the winding roads of this beautiful country to understand why so many Sicilians left the island and came to America.

To comprehend the problems facing a driver in Sicily, one must first take note of what can be found on the Sicilian highway during the course of a day's drive. There are, and not necessarily in this order, four-cylinder Fiats, eight-cylinder Ferraris, twelve-cylinder Alfa Romeos, hay trucks, gasoline trucks, motorcycles, motor scooters, bicycles, horse-drawn wagons, donkey carts, hand-drawn carts, dogs, goats, sheep, chickens, children, fishermen, members of the clergy, *carabinieri* and highway bandits.

Sicilians by tradition are contemptuous of the other fellow's means of transportation and there is a continual vendetta going on among all the vehicles on the road. It has been said that the dreaded members of the Mafia are boy scouts compared to the people who have drivers' licenses in Sicily.

For one thing the traditional *omertà*, or conspiracy of silence, that Sicilians are known for does not apply to anything that happens on the road. When one Sicilian passes another he will shout at him that he is a fool, an idiot and his mother was a goat, and, if really angered, that his father was a policeman. The man passed will retort with words of equal passion and will, if the wind is right, spit at the other car. Since Sicilians must use their hands when making expressive statements, neither driver has his hands on the wheel when yelling at the other.

If there are other passengers in the cars, they, too, will join in the argument. Even after the man who is doing the passing has made the maneuver, he will look back, waving both hands at the driver he has passed, who in turn will retort by either waving his hands or pressing the horn for as long as the battery will allow.

The only place one Sicilian will pass another Sicilian is on a curve. Occasionally a car or truck will be coming the other way and then the driver faces what is know in Sicily as "the moment of truth." If he swerves to avoid the oncoming car he will be considered a coward and his whole family will be in disgrace. He must force the other car to swerve. To see two brave men meeting face to face on a Sicilian highway is a sight one will never forget.

The one thing that can slow up a Sicilian driver is a donkey cart. All the donkey carts in Sicily are beautifully painted with pictures of knights in armor and scenes of great battles. Drivers of donkey carts get most of their sleep on the roads of Sicily and the donkeys seem to also. A donkey cart can be found on any side of a Sicilian road, going in any direction. Although the carts themselves only take up one lane, the hay the carts carry is purposely laid horizontally across them, taking up two or sometimes three lanes, thus making it impossible for anyone to see what is happening up ahead. Donkey drivers are used to the sound of automobile horns and can rarely be waked up by one. The best thing you can do when you're caught behind a donkey cart is to relax and enjoy the painted pictures.

It is an accepted fact that when a Sicilian car is approaching a village, the driver speeds up and presses his hand on the horn as hard as he can. But instead of frightening the villagers, it has exactly the opposite effect. Children rush out of their houses at the sound of a horn and start playing in the streets, dogs out minding sheep rush into town to find out what is going on, and chickens start crossing the road to get to the other side.

The driver who has his honor at stake refuses to slow down and the village population refuses to get out of his way. I can't tell you how it is possible for a car to get through a village without hitting anything since I've always had my eyes closed when I've gone through one.

Besides all the other hazards of driving in Sicily, there is one that is slowly dying out, and that is highway robbery. Sicily has always been noted for its famed highwaymen, who stuck up cars presumably to rob from the rich to give to the poor. But, like the Marshall plan, the money rarely filtered down to the people who really needed it.

There are still some highway robberies committed and it's very wise for a stranger when asking directions in one of the towns which is noted for its bandits to ask how to get to a town which is in the opposite direction from the one to which he is going. Anyone who indicates which road he is taking is just asking for trouble, and if he's driving in Sicily he's got enough as it is.

Before we take you on a tour of all the places you're going to wish you were going to, and a few you'll be glad you're missing, we'd like to give you a few overviews of Italy by three extremely perceptive humorists: S. J. Perelman—a globetrotter who took Mark Twain into the twentieth century, and beyond—trots, or rather gallups, through Italy just after World War Two had ended; George Mikes doesn't bother with name brands, but instead gives us a look at the generic Italian town; and Charles Dickens sums things up, as usual.

S. J. Perelman
An Agonizing Chronicle 1947

IT DID NOT REQUIRE an especially perceptive nature to sense from the moment we tied up at Naples the sadness and dilapidation of the city. Great stretches of dockside and industrial district were still in ruins, and the population, or what remnant was visible in the echoing, poorly lighted streets, seemed malnourished and despairing. Perhaps it was this heavy oppressiveness, aggravated by the rumor that the ship might be detained there, that stampeded me into joining the excursion I did. If I had suspected its true scope, or the complete naïveté of trying to cover a major portion of Italy in four days, I might have harkened to Hirschfeld and sailed with him to Genoa. But then, that would have been sagacious, and sagacity has never been my long suit.

On the surface, to one who had never been in the country, our itinerary appeared perfectly feasible—Pompeii, Rome, Siena, Florence, Pisa, and on to Genoa by the Italian Riviera. In the big red Fiat bus with me that sparkling morning went eight other innocents—Wickwire and Chung, the intrepid duo who had helped me solve the riddle of the Great Pyramid; Mr. Sabadhai, a pursy Indian textile magnate, and his wife; Azeez, a sniveling young Bengali on his way to Johns Hopkins to study dentistry; the Beavers, a well-heeled elderly couple from Lake Forest; and Miss Gorsline, a spinsterish New England schoolteacher. In charge of the flock, and none too elated with his assignment, was a peppery, disenchanted Neapolitan named Mr. Frascati, whose expression of choler hardly deserted him from the instant he saw us. He considered the expedition unmitigated lunar idiocy, and I must say nothing happened to disprove him.

We tore through Pompeii in a dog-trot, frantically snatching postcards and marveling dutifully at the reconstructions; anyone who showed a tendency to browse was quickly shooed along by Frascati, who made it clear the schedule allowed no time for giggling over erotica. By midday we were boiling through the Apennine hill towns at a terrifying rate, in our wake a series of moribund chickens and peasants screaming maledictions. The scenery was spectacular: endless rolling vineyards under full cultivation, medieval villages perched on the most outlandish crags, superb perspectives of cypresses and Lombardy poplars outlined against the sky. At Viterbo, a somnolent mountain hamlet out of a Shubert operetta, we dallied long enough to gulp down a flask of memorable white wine and allow a bullock to trample on my foot and thundered on. The havoc caused by bombs and shellfire, sporadic until now, became truly appalling at the Volturno. The destruction was so overwhelming that you wondered how men found the courage to face the task of rebuilding; and yet there, as everywhere along the Via Appia, were constant evidences of a tenacious, energetic rehabilitation. No monument or shrine I saw in central Italy, and I was fated to see nearly all of them, was half as impressive as the dogged industry with which the people were restoring their homes and workshops.

There is a pungent old Calabrian proverb, whose meaning I have forgotten if I ever knew it, which states that the human spinal column can stand a powerful lot of abuse. Mine certainly served as a whipping boy that day. Long after dark, spent and nerve-weary, I doddered into the foyer of a third-rate hotel in Rome, was fed as wretched a meal of rubbery veal and warmed-over spaghetti as a swindling management could confect on short notice, and was bivouacked in a disused storeroom. My slumber was a mite less than refreshing; Azeez, my Indian bunkmate, dreamt he was being crushed by the Juggernaut and howled like a timber wolf all night long.

The next morning found us on the treadmill in earnest; paced by Frascati, we sprinted through the mile-long corridors of the Vatican, gaped at Michelangelo's murals in the Sistine Chapel, goggled at the immensity of St. Peter's. After lunch, Wickwire and I made a desperate attempt to vamoose, but the guide had been ordered to show us Rome and show it he did. Borghese Gardens, the Roman Forum, the Colosseum, the Piazza Venezia, and the gigantic cheese fondant commemorating Victor Emmanuel. Somewhere in the midst of these architectural glories, my feet ceased to function as organs of locomotion and I finished the day *hors de combat*, numbly festooned over Frascati and Wickwire in the humiliating posture known as the fireman's carry. With admirable presence of mind, they dragged me to a small surgery on the Corso, where my jaws were pried open with a sharp stick and a shakerful of martinis introduced, and soon I was reeling back to my hotel, yodeling *La Traviata* as good as new.

It would serve no useful purpose to prolong the agonizing chronicle of our hegira; once established, the hallucinatory pattern intensified like that of a six-day bicycle race. Out of the nightmare I remember isolated highlights: a truly symphonic dish of green noodles in Siena, the panorama of Tuscan hills that was purest primitive painting, the theatrical splendor of Florence, the breath-taking Byzantine mosaics in the cathedral at Pisa, a lunch deserving of the Cordon Bleu in a tiny restaurant in Viareggio. Interthreaded through it is the recollection of unending heat and dust, of a blurred succession of churches, fountains, and largely hideous sculpture, and the tireless clack of Miss Gorsline's tongue as she annotated the wonders whirling by us. When we reached the Italian Riviera at last, the driver cast discretion to the winds and decided to give us a farewell *frisson*. All his southern Latin daredeviltry rose to the surface; throttle wide open, rocking and careering around horrid chasms, the bus hurtled down the precipitous coast past La Spezia and Rapallo as though Beelzebub himself were at the controls. Our homecoming created a minor sensation aboard the *President Polk* and provided touching proof, if any was necessary, of the esteem our mates felt for us. So sure had everyone been that we would never return alive that our effects had been auctioned off among the passengers. I consumed a whole day retrieving my wardrobe from other people's cabins and had many piquant adventures, none of them, however, pertinent to this narrative.

George Mikes
The Town 1956

LEAVING THE CATHEDRAL, cross the square and turn sharp left. You must not fail to make an intensive tour of the town which is one of the most beautiful and ancient towns in Italy. It was built as an Etruscan village but during Roman times it was inhabited mostly by Romans. After the downfall of Rome, it was occupied by the barbarians from the North, then by the barbarians from the East and later by the barbarians from the North again. In the 10th and 11th centuries it was the battleground of feuding lords. In the 12th century it became an independent Republic and to celebrate its independence a large number of heretics were burnt alive in the market square. The town was occupied by Napoleon who put one of his brothers on the throne; later it was occupied by the Austrians who were succeeded by the French who were succeeded by the Austrians. The Republic joined the Kingdom of Italy in 1860.

A large number of buildings which have survived centuries of strife and destruction are veritable masterpieces: a large number of other buildings which have not survived were also veritable masterpieces. In the third street on the right you find the *Museo* (Museum, really) containing one of the finest art collections in Italy. Coming out of the *Museo* turn sharp right again and go down the beautiful Renaissance marble staircase; turn sharp left and come up again. In the Church of San Giovanni (one of the finest Renaissance churches in Italy) you can see Tintoretto's masterpiece, "Madonna with Four Saints". In the Church of San Giacomo you can see Botticelli's masterpiece, "Two Saints with the Madonna". In the Church of San Bartolomeo do not miss Tiepolo's hugh canvas, "Madonna with Twenty Three Saints". In the chapel of San Marco, the focus of attention is Perugino's small painting, "Madonna with Just One Saint".

Admission to most of these churches is free except for the few hundred lire you are expected to give the priest at the main door. (Useless trying the side door, there is another priest there.)

(In Rome, in the church of San Pietro in Vincoli—the home of Michelangelo's Moses—a priest stops you to enquire: why do you wish to go in? Should you say: to see Moses, you are required to pay 200 lire which sum, however, is not an entrance fee but a voluntary contribution on your part. If your intention is to pray, entrance is free. If you want to go in both to pray and to see Moses, you pay half price.)

Proceeding towards the right you reach the fortress built between 1254 and 1355. Now it is used as a Museum (*Museo,* in Italian). Opposite is the Palazzo, ancient home of the Podesta, now used as a Museum. The next building on the right is the old Museum, now used as a Palazzo.

Leaving the Palazzo, you enter the Old Town which is extremely Mediæval with a dash of Renaissance. In the Old Town, as well as in all the outlying districts, you can see a number of romantic people. Most of them are very hungry which is also romantic. They are clad in picturesque rags which in winter time become even more picturesque. Many of these people have a romantic smell.

Then you stop to think a little. Most of the riches and beauty of Italy have been handed down from ancient times. Not all, of course: Italian opera—to mention only one example—is a recent phenomenon. Yet, on the whole, apart from Italy's natural beauty which is eternal, her man-made beauty consists either of Roman ruins or else art-treasures the most recent of which are 300 years old. No country can match Italy's wealth; and few countries can match Italy's poverty. The problem the Italians seem to have solved with such dazzling and stupefying brilliance is this: How to remain poor on a rich inheritance?

Charles Dickens
Extremes 1844

MY VERY DEAR MAC—I address you with something of the lofty spirit of an exile—a banished commoner—a sort of Anglo-Pole. I don't exactly know what I have done for my country in coming away from it; but I feel it is something—something great—something virtuous and heroic. Lofty emotions rise within me, when I see the sun set on the blue Mediterranean. I am the limpet on the rock. My father's name is Turner, and my boots are green.

Apropos of blue. In a certain picture, called "The Serenade," you painted a sky. If you ever have occasion to paint the Mediterranean, let it be exactly of that colour. It lies before me now, as deeply and intensely blue. But no such colour is above me. Nothing like it. In the South of France—at Avignon, at Aix, at Marseilles—I saw deep blue skies (not so deep though—O Lord, no!), and also in America; but the sky above me is familiar to my sight. Is it heresy to say that I have seen its twin brother shining through the window of Jack Straw's—that down in

Devonshire I have seen a better sky? I dare say it is; but like a great many other heresies, it is true.

But such green—green—green—as flutters in the vineyard down below the windows, *that* I never saw; nor yet such lilac, and such purple as float between me and the distant hills; nor yet—in anything—picture, book, or verbal boredom—such awful, solemn, impenetrable blue, as is that same sea. It has such an absorbing, silent, deep, profound effect, that I can't help thinking it suggested the idea of Styx. It looks as if a draught of it—only so much as you could scoop up on the beach, in the hollow of your hand—would wash out everything else, and make a great blue blank of your intellect.

When the sun sets clearly, then, by Heaven, it is majestic! From any one of eleven windows here, or from a terrace overgrown with grapes, you may behold the broad sea; villas, houses, mountains, forts, strewn with rose-leaves—strewn with thorns—stifled in thorns! Dyed through and through and through. For a moment. No more. The sun is impatient and fierce, like everything else in these parts, and goes down headlong. Run to fetch your hat—and it's night. Wink at the right time of black night—and it's morning. Everything is in extremes. There is an insect here (I forget its name, and Fletcher and Roche are both out) that chirps all day. There is one outside the window now. The chirp is very loud, something like a Brobdingnagian grasshopper. The creature is born to chirp—to progress in chirping—to chirp louder, louder, louder—till it gives one tremendous chirp, and bursts itself. That is its life and death. Everything "is in a concatenation accordingly." The day gets brighter, brighter, brighter, till it's night. The summer gets hotter, hotter, hotter, till it bursts. The fruit gets riper, riper, riper, till it tumbles down and rots.

*The North

*Northern Italy has everything: art, fashion, lakes, meadows, heavy industry in the valleys and light air up in the Alps. Despite the boot's crest of fringe up the side and its famous volcanoes in the south, it is hard to believe that the highest point of Europe is in Italy or, at least, at its border with France. No wonder Switzerland and Austria have had to make such a big deal out of their puny molehills they call The Alps! What they don't want to get out is that not only are theirs smaller, but they've got all the northern faces, while Italy basks in the palm-treed paradise of the southern exposures. Ah, to sit lakeside under a palm tree and sip a Caribbean cocktail while looking up at the snow-crested Alps. Unfortunately, there's not much humor in that; only a bit of quiet, perhaps snobbish joy.

No, in northern Italy you have to seek out your humor in the Big Fig, Milan, home of everything fashionable; in the home of the national symbol, Pisa; in the shore resorts; and in Genoa, home of Christopher Columbus, who needed a Spanish purse to discover the Italians' second home. We are fortunate to have the delightful Czechoslovak writer Karel Capek and his American counterpart in delightfulness Emily Kimbrough to give us their appreciations of the metropolis known as Milan, after which Mark Twain gives us his own special recipe for truly enjoying a sightseeing tour of Columbus's Genoa.

Karel Capek
Milan 1929

AND THEN I SAW a Babelesquian tower where languages have been confused for five centuries, i.e., Milan Cathedral. From a distance it looks like a gigantic piece of dazzling antimony that crystalizes into slender needles, or like an anxious marble artichoke; every needle is a little spire or clove, and when you split one it is full of statues piled on statues, which can only be seen by climbing the roof. There are only 2,300 of these statues, or so Baedeker states in figures always very conservative, but I don't think he counted the small figures in relief. The cathedral is one of the greatest aberrations I have ever seen; it will bewilder you with the extent of its fantasies. The statues certainly aren't worth much, its feathered arches are parched, the needles and steeples are senseless, but so is the whole thing, so in the end it relies entirely on its fantastic, crazy, ghostly intemperance.

But there are some churches, bathed in shadow, venerable, and cheery, e.g., Sant' Ambrogio or San Lorenzo, where much has remained of the red-haired Lombards; others are decorated by sweet Luini; and yet others are charmingly and severely Bramantesque; but all these have nothing to do with the Milan of today. Milan, the most populous of Italian princedoms, wants itself considered a little London. Therefore, there are myriads of carriages, motors, confounded bicycles, noises, banks, colporteurs, tramways, marble lavatories, illuminated signs, people and bustle, and guardians of the peace with black helmets who look like undertakers' assistants, and commerce, yelling, haste, and all possible things. The people there are godless, they don't keep saints' days and they even disregard other traditions, such as *lazzaroni*, mendicancy, and picturesqueness. They do not sleep on the footpaths, or hang their laundry in the streets, or knock cattle about, or sew boots in the middle of the street, or sing *barcarolles:* in fact they do nothing picturesque, and so one can breathe better there, since even the atmosphere of the glorious past is gone.

Emily Kimbrough
Scattered Like Leaves 1954

THE INSTANT OUR BAGGAGE WAS DELIVERED to us we left the hotel for a walk. I can report nothing of whatever places of interest there may be between the Palace Hotel and the Cathedral of Milan, but I can set down with underlining that the traffic at five-thirty in that section of Milan makes the cars on Madison Avenue at that hour a sedate procession taking their occupants to church. Five minutes after we had begun our walk there was no hunger left in me for the beauty of the Milan Cathedral. The only thing that drove me on to see it was the impossibility of turning back to the safety of the Palace Hotel, though I longed to take refuge there. On the sidewalk pedestrians whirled us half-way around and others back again as if the three of us were "it" in Blind Man's Bluff. On the curb the pedals of passing bicycles nicked our shins, and in the streets to which we were pushed from the rear, motorists played "one, two, three, and down goes she" with the three of us. I suppose Italian cars have brakes, unless as a measure of postwar economy they are omitted as foolish luxuries. But I venture to wager if they are still included in the equipment of an automobile, a used car is turned in with the brake as fresh as the day it left the factory. The horn and the accelerator get the hardest wear.

At one crossing, Sophy, Zella and I scattered like leaves before an autumn wind. I came to rest in a little haven between two parked cars, and I sat down on the bumper of one because my knees were chattering. From my retreat I peeked out cautiously dreading the possible sight of my friends, or parts of them, scattered about the street. Mercifully there was no evidence of such dissolution, but I saw an Italian traffic policeman, and that is a pretty sight. I don't know where these officers receive their training; from the Sadler's Wells Ballet School, I should think. Beyond the first one I spotted I caught sight of a fellow officer on a near-by intersection giving a duplicate performance.

A "stop" was indicated by the left hand smacked smartly against the thigh; the right hand straight ahead in the manner of a duelist's thrust, except with the hand up, palm out. Permission for traffic from the right to advance was indicated by first the left arm above the head, palm out. That halted traffic from the left. Then with the right arm softly curved, in the kind of sweeping motion I used to make when, playing jacks, I executed the maneuver called "pigs in a pen," he coaxed toward him the traffic on his right. To stop the traffic on either side in order to allow intersecting lines to cross, this artist crossed arms over his breast, and then as if on an inner count of two, extended his arms, at either side with palm out and with drama in every widespread finger. I was sorry to see no leaping nor twinkle-toes. Perhaps footwork is postgraduate study.

What I did see, however, were my friends safe on a sidewalk, but running up and down it, evidently searching for me. Their concern forced me from my sanctuary. I ventured out, and in a series of the sort of leaps I had hoped to see the policeman make, I reached my dear ones, and we shook hands all around in mutual congratulations and thanksgiving that, though nervously impaired, we were physically intact.

131

Mark Twain
Making It Interesting 1869

OUR GUIDE HAS MARCHED US through miles of pictures and sculpture in the vast corridors of the Vatican; and through miles of pictures and sculpture in twenty other palaces; he has shown us the great picture in the Sistine Chapel, and frescoes enough to frescoe the heavens—pretty much all done by Michael Angelo. So with him we have played that game which has vanquished so many guides for us—imbecility and idiotic questions. These creatures never suspect—they have no idea of a sarcasm.

He shows us a figure and says: "Statoo brunzo." (Bronze statue.)

We look at it indifferently and the doctor asks: "By Michael Angelo?"

"No—not know who."

Then he shows us the ancient Roman Forum. The doctor asks: "Michael Angelo?"

A stare from the guide. "No—thousan' year before he is born."

Then an Egyptian obelisk. Again: "Michael Angelo?"

"Oh, *mon dieu,* genteelmen! Zis is *two* thousan' year before he is born!"

He grows so tired of that unceasing question sometimes, that he dreads to show us any thing at all. The wretch has tried all the ways he can think of to make us comprehend that Michael Angelo is only responsible for the creation of a part of the world, but somehow he has not succeeded yet. Relief for overtasked eyes and brain from study and sight-seeing is necessary, or we shall become idiotic sure enough. Therefore this guide must continue to suffer. If he does not enjoy it, so much the worse for him. We do.

In this place I may as well jot down a chapter concerning those necessary nuisances, European guides. Many a man has wished in his heart he could do without his guide; but knowing he could not, has wished he could get some amusement out of him as a remuneration for the affliction of his society. We accomplished this latter matter, and if our experience can be made useful to others they are welcome to it.

Guides know about enough English to tangle every thing up so that a man can make neither head or tail of it. They know their story by heart—the history of every statue, painting, cathedral or other wonder they show you. They know it and tell it as a parrot would—and if you interrupt, and throw them off the track, they have to go back and begin over again. All their lives long, they are employed in showing strange things to foreigners and listening to their bursts of admiration. It is human nature to take delight in exciting admiration. It is what prompts children to say "smart" things, and do absurd ones, and in other ways "show off" when company is present. It is what makes gossips turn out in rain and storm to go and be the first to tell a startling bit of news. Think, then, what a passion it becomes with a guide, whose privilege it is, every day, to show to strangers wonders that throw them into perfect ecstasies of admiration! He gets so that he could not by any possibility live in a soberer atmosphere. After we discovered this, we *never* went into ecstacies any more—we never admired any thing—we never showed any but impassible faces and stupid indifference in the presence of the sublimest wonders a guide had to display. We had found their weak point. We have made good use of it ever since. We have made some of those people savage, at times, but we have never lost our own serenity.

The doctor asks the questions, generally, because he can keep his countenance, and look more like an inspired idiot, and throw more imbecility into the tone of his voice than any man that lives. It comes natural to him.

The guides in Genoa are delighted to secure an American party, because Americans so much wonder, and deal so much in sentiment and emotion before any relic of Columbus. Our guide there fidgeted about as if he had swallowed a spring mattress. He was full of animation—full of impatience. He said:

"Come wis me, genteelmen!—come! I show you ze letter writing by Christopher Colombo!—write it himself!—write it wis his own hand!—come!"

He took us to the municipal palace. After much impressive fumbling of keys and opening of locks, the stained and aged document was spread before us. The guide's eyes sparkled. He danced about us and tapped the parchment with his finger:

"What I tell you, genteelmen! Is it not so! See! handwriting Christopher Colombo!—write it himself!"

We looked indifferent—unconcerned. The doctor examined the document very deliberately, during a painful pause.—Then he said, without any show of interest:

"Ah—Ferguson—what—what did you say was the name of the party who wrote this?"

"Christopher Colombo! ze great Christopher Colombo!"

Another deliberate examination.

"Ah—did he write it himself, or—or how?"

"He write it himself!—Christopher Colombo! he's own hand-writing, write by himself!"

Then the doctor laid the document down and said:

"Why, I have seen boys in America only fourteen years old that could write better than that."

"But zis is ze great Christo—"

"I don't care who it is! It's the worst writing I ever saw. Now you mustn't think you can impose on us because we are strangers. We are not fools, by a good deal. If you have got any specimens of penmanship of real merit, trot them out!—and if you haven't, drive on!"

We drove on. The guide was considerably shaken up, but he made one more venture. He had something which he thought would overcome us. He said:

"Ah, genteelmen, you come wis me! I show you beautiful, O, magnificent bust Christoper Colombo!—splendid, grand, magnificent!"

He brought us before the beautiful bust—for it *was* beautiful—and sprang back and struck an attitude:

"Ah, look, genteelmen!—beautiful, grand,—bust Christopher Colombo!—beautiful bust, beautiful pedestal!"

The doctor put up his eye-glass—procured for such occasions:

"Ah—what did you say this gentleman's name was?"

"Christopher Colombo!—ze great Christopher Colombo!"

"Christopher Colombo—the great Christopher Colombo. Well, what did *he* do?"

"Discover America!—discover America, Oh, ze devil!"

"Discover America. No—that statement will hardly wash. We are just from America ourselves. We heard nothing about it. Christopher Colombo—pleasant name—is—is he dead?"

"Oh, *corpo di Baccho!*—three hundred year!"

"What did he die of?"

"I do not know!—I can not tell."

"Small-pox, think?"

"I do not know, genteelmen!—I do not know what he die of!"

"Measles, likely?"

"May be—may be—I do *not* know—I think he die of somethings."

"Parents living?"

"Im-posseeble!"

"Ah—which is the bust and which is the pedestal?"

"Santa Maria!—*zis* ze bust!—*zis* ze pedestal!"

"Ah, I see, I see—happy combination—very happy combination, indeed. Is—is this the first time this gentleman was ever on a bust?"

That joke was lost on the foreigner—guides can not master the subtleties of the American joke.

Is there any other country in the world whose symbol, at least for the tourist, does not lie in one of its major tourist destinations? The Statue of Liberty's in New York, Big Ben's in London, the Eiffel Tower's in Paris, and the Kremlin's in Moscow. The Tower of Pisa's in Pisa, to be sure, but where is Pisa? Thirty-five miles down the Arno from Florence. (By the way, the Arno's importance to the world of humor has nothing to do with its passage through these heralded cities; rather, it is famous for having loaned its name to the great cartoonist Peter Arno.) In other words, Galileo foresaw that Pisa would be only a daytrip away from a tourist hub. A necessary daytrip, too, for how can you really be sure it leans unless you visit it yourself? How else can you go home and tell the neighbors how long you think it'll be before a strong gust helps what made it famous—gravity—do its thing? Here's a rushed tour of the venerable town by the unfortunate P. G. Konody.

P. G. Konody
Sniffing at Pisa 1911

OUR ROAD FOLLOWED THE RAILWAY through the valley by which the Serchio River breaks through the wooded hills that form an almost complete circle around Lucca. A happy, smiling, fertile, and well-cultivated country, with alternating cornfields, mulberry and olive plantations, and maize fields. However, we had not proceeded ten miles on the winding road, when the sunny sky lost its smile and assumed a threatening frown, followed by some heavy tears which made us stop to put up the Cape-hood. It was just what one might have expected. Does Pisa ever enjoy a day of unbroken sunshine? Possibly, or it could not have been described with the degree of exalted enthusiasm with which its vaunted charms have been belauded by some of its admirers. But to me the charming side of Pisa was and remains a sealed book. I had tried to break the seal on four previous occasions, and each time I got drenched to the skin. And Pisa is quite peculiarly unpleasant in rainy weather. It is more depressing than any other Italian town I have visited in similar conditions. Pisa in rain is enough to ruffle the sweetest temper and to make honeymooners quarrel.

By the time we had passed Bagni S. Giuliano and swung round into the fine straight avenue of over three miles in length that leads to the Porta Lucca, rain was pouring down in torrents, and we were all quite ready to be annoyed with Pisa. Instead of entering by the Lucca gate, I made Ryder turn to the right along the old city walls, the northwest corner of which encloses the famous *fabbriche*, and take us round the Jewish cemetery to the Porta Nuova, which leads straight into the Piazza del Duomo, the "glory of Pisa." There was no sunlight to bring out the warmth of the time-worn marble, and to accentuate the architectural articulation and elegant details by the play of cast shadows; but still the Duomo, planted on a vast grassy plot between the Baptistery and the Leaning Tower, with the Campo Santo and the mediæval city wall in the background, was a sight to force a shout of admiration even from unwilling throats. * * *

I have no wish to compete with the excellent guidebooks that give an exhaustive account of the artistic riches heaped up in this corner of Pisa. The importance of Niccolo Pisano's great pulpit of 1360 for the whole evolution of Italian art is a matter of common knowledge. But we were not in an appreciative mood. We were more struck by the illogical absurdity of the supporting columns being placed on the backs of walking lions—a motive often repeated in Romanesque art—than by the beauty of the whole fabric and by the classic sense of form and movement in the relief figures on the walls of the hexagonal pulpit-box. That we had to submit to the undesired explanations of a guide who had attached himself to our little party added to our irritability. I knew the man was waiting for his supreme *coup*—the wonderful echo of the Baptistery, in which imaginative writers have discovered the voices of the angelic choir. For the guide that echo spelt more *soldi* than all the marble miracles wrought by the Pisani; and he certainly knew how to pitch his voice so as to get the most effective response from the masonry of the lofty dome, which the reverberating sound seemed to lift into space. It was an echo that suggested a moving geometrical pattern of interlaced curves. It did not seem to be thrown back from the walls, but rather made the massive masonry sway in gentle movement. Still, we did not admit any surprise, and made for the door before the guide had finished his vocal recital.

The Campo Santo was our next objective. I was all eagerness to renew acquaintance after so many years with the "solemn loveliness" of this sequestered plot of cypress-planted sacred earth shut in by an ambulatory with colonnades of exquisite Gothic tracery; and with the famous Roman sarcophagus from which Niccolo Pisano drew his inspiration; and with the faded splendour of its sadly deteriorated frescoes—those much-debated early paintings of the *Triumph of Death* and the *Last Judgment*, which the best modern expert opinion has given to the Sienese brothers Lorenzetti and their pupils, and the vast series of genre-like scriptural subjects, in which Benozzo Gozzoli has left for future generations a living representation of the life of his own days. We waded across to the turnstile at the entrance to the Campo Santo, and tendered coin of the realm to the doorkeeper. He shook his head and cut figures through the air with the waving forefinger of his right hand. He was not allowed to take money at the gate. We would have to obtain tickets at some place right at the other end of the *piazza*. Could he send for the tickets? No, he had no one to send. Arguments were of no avail. After a brief consultation we decided not to submit to so unnecessary a piece of chicanery, told the incorruptible uniformed Cerberus what we thought of Pisan red-tape, and hurried back to the western gates of the Duomo.

By now we had become possessed of the real Pisan temper, and I fear the beggars at the church door did not reap the harvest they expected. The *fabbriche* had lost their charm; the Baptistery looked more than ever like a pepper-pot; the facade of the Duomo was no better, if not worse, than that of many a church in Lucca; the interior annoyed us by its zebra stripes of black and white marble; the pictures, with the exception of the "modernised" Byzantinesque mosaic once attributed to Cimabue, were mostly of too late a date to enlist our interest, and the Leaning Tower seemed more drunk and freakish than ever. We simply walked through the Duomo more to keep our feet dry than to see anything in particular; and five minutes after our dispute with the Campo Santo guardian we were again in our wonted places in the car, driving over the wet flagstones of the Via Solferino to the Arno Bridge, and then through the southern quarter of the town to the old fortress and the Porta Florentina.

Not a word was spoken as we sped along, between a railway on the right and a tram-line on the left, on a wretched, shaky road in the direction of Florence. Then suddenly I was startled from a resentful reverie by an explosion of cackling sound behind me. It was Pomponius literally rocking and swaying with laughter, gasping for breath, and then firing off a second volley. He had realised the humour of the situation, and enjoyed the joke for some time before he was able to blurt out an answer to satisfy our curiosity.

"Sniffing at Pisa! literally sniffing at Pisa! Has anybody ever heard of such snobbery? To come a thousand miles and more by car to see Pisa, and then just to sniff at it! He! he!" And he was seized by another fit of explosive hilarity.

Although it's not quite as well known as its French counterpart on the other side of Monaco, the Italian Riviera is far better known than the Adriatic shore, at least to us readers of English-language fiction and watchers of English-language films. But the Adriatic coast is to the Italian what Brighton is to the Briton and what the Jersey Shore is to the northeast American. In other words, if you want to see how the other 80% lives, it might be worth a try. Here's English poet Donald Hall on a rarely-visited sight in Rimini, a near-suburb of the miniature nation of San Marino (the miniature nations, by the way, seem too small for humorists to make fun of them; they're not bullies, you know!).

Donald Hall
How Do You Get In? 1956

RIMINI IS THE BRIGHTON OF THE ADRIATIC, and in summer, Germans and Italians from the northern cities pour into its hundreds of hotels and *pensione;* but all that area stretching as far as the eye can see along the coast is divided from the Old City by the main north-south railway and sidings. For that reason the town of the Malatestas, who were not concerned with sun-bathing and did their building a good mile from the sea, was almost untouched in the last war. The Allied armies advancing along the coast were interested mainly in the railway, the bridges and the Port Canal, and in the course of their advance obliterated the miles of seaside resort. The speed with which it has been almost wholly rebuilt is astounding.

I liked the grey arcaded streets of the Old Town and the rather tough-looking people who seemed in no particular hurry about anything now that they were able to live their own lives for a while without bothering about visitors. Near the south-west gate on the far side of an enormous *piazza*, that even now looked as though purposely cleared to prevent surprise attack, stood the Rocca Malatestiana, without exception the grimmest medieval fortess I have ever seen. Its high walls surrounded several acres with no break in them but massive iron grilles. The door in the crenellated tower facing the *piazza* looked so small that I did not believe it could be the main entrance, but after walking all round I could see no other. So I went over to a man who was unloading some vegetables from a cart and asked him if I could go in.

"That depends," he said, "if you've any relatives inside."

I replied that I had not, but why was that important? He admitted that sometimes friends were allowed in, but only with special permission. "In any event you are made to empty your pockets. I know because I used to go in, though I never saw much."

If he had gone in there seemed no reason why I couldn't.

"But you're different," he said. "I had a brother there, he was there for two years, the walls are eight-foot thick."

"Was he a guide, or a custodian or something of the sort?"

"A what?" The man looked at me and began to shake with laughter. "Haven't you read the notice?"

He was so overcome that I left him to try on my own. There was a piece of paper, so small that I had not noticed it, pinned on a door that appeared to have neither handle nor key-hole. "Relatives of the prisoners may be admitted between 15 and 18 hours." The man waved to me as I turned away. "Go and steal something," he called. "But it's harder still to get out."

The South

There is so much south of Italy and so little time. There may be fewer art treasures, but they are more than made up for by mountains such as Vesuvius and Etna, by islands such as Sicily and Capri, by rarely visited areas like Apulia and Calabria, heel and toe, respectively. Not to mention, of course, Rome and Naples. The south is home to what most of us think of as Italian food as well as to what most of us think of as Italians.

But where does the South start? Where is the line where the tomatoes and the olive oil really begin to flow? In the first selection, the man with all the solutions, George Mikes, tells us the answer. Then we will hear about the ancient city of Naples, the flashy island of Capri, the fabled ruins of Pompeii, the most infamous denizens of Sicily, and the awful catacombs of Palermo from the likes of Mark Twain; the delightful artist, novelist, travel and children's writer Ludwig Bemelmans; travel writer John Gibbons; Mr Punch; and J. Ross Browne, the American who made the humorous travelogue fashionable there, only to be soon overshadowed by Mark Twain, and then forgotten.

George Mikes
The Line 1956

IN ITALY PEOPLE TALK a great deal about the Line—
meaning the sharp and clearly perceptible dividing
Line between North and South Italy. Some put the Line
north of Rome, others a little to the south of it. Some say
that at a definite point you suddenly leave modern, industrial Europe and find yourself in the Middle East with
its donkeys, orange groves and palm-trees. The Line has
many different names and this I found rather confusing.
I am pleased to report that I can clear the matter up. The
Line runs actually right through Rome and its correct
name is: the *Parker 51 Line*.

It was at the Spanish Steps in Rome that I first became
aware of its existence. A blonde English girl of distinction
and charm—the type that never utters a harsh word and
never raises her voice even at Wimbledon Centre Court—
was standing there, her eyes flashing and, her face suf-
fused with passion, she foamed at the mouth as she
screamed at a gentleman who had just spoken to her:

"No, I do *not* want a Parker 51."

I looked at her in amazement.

"Poor girl," I remarked to my wife. "Off her head!"

But I found out soon enough that she was not off her
head. We had hardly walked thirty steps when a
gentleman approached me and declared:

"I have a Parker 51 for sale. Only two dollars."

I declined with thanks. He walked on by my side ex-
tolling the virtues of the pen. When I persisted in my
refusal, he offered me Swiss watches, Dutch gin, a con-
signment of dried fruit and a new kind of rubber sponge.
This conversation was repeated about two hundred times
a day.

The situation really became a little irritating when we reached Naples.

There I stopped a gentleman to ask the way to Corso Garibaldi. He told me that he would gladly give me the required information if I bought a Parker 51 from him. Two dollars only. Very good. Very cheap.

In three hours in Naples I could have bought about 400 Parker 51 pens; I was urged to visit about three dozen restaurants; I was practically dragged into three churches and five horse-drawn carriages for sightseeing tours. Seven people offered to take our photograph, more than fifty regaled us with truly beautiful Neapolitan songs and whenever we approached a door, about nine people opened it for us and bowed deeply. The crisis came in Pompeii where as I passed a public convenience, a lady emerged and invited me to try out her establishment, emphasising its incomparable advantages over her nearest competitor.

That was a little too much for me.

We jumped into the car and drove southward—away from people, away from so-called civilisation, away from Parker 51s. We reached Sorrento where hordes of hotel-porters dressed in police-like uniforms tried to stop us and drag us into their hotels or at least their restaurants. When we did not stop they shouted after us that they had Parker 51s for sale.

We passed through Sorrento and reached a tiny village nearby. Not a single porter tried to abduct us so—for that very reason—we stopped and took a room. When we went out for a walk the porter, dressed like a policeman, was busy in front of the hotel, trying to stop cars.

We started walking briskly and walked for an hour till we reached the top of a cliff—a kind of terrace over the sea. There was a priest deep in prayer among the rocks taking no notice of us, indeed, of the material world around him. Below us rolled the deep blue sea, above us stretched the deep blue sky; around us towered the great bare rocks and in front of us knelt a priest in deep and pious prayer. Here, at last, everything was peace and quiet.

I was lost in the sheer, enthralling beauty of the place.

Suddenly I started. Someone was talking to me. It was the priest. He had a deep, mellifluous voice. He said:

"I have a Parker 51 for sale. Two dollars only. Very good. Very cheap."

Mark Twain
See Naples and Die 1869

SEE NAPLES AND DIE." Well, I do not know that one would necessarily die after merely seeing it, but to attempt to live there might turn out a little differently. To see Naples as we saw it in the early dawn from far up on the side of Vesuvius, is to see a picture of wonderful beauty. At that distance its dingy buildings looked white—and so, rank on rank of balconies, windows and roofs, they piled themselves up from the blue ocean till the colossal castle of St. Elmo topped the grand white pyramid and gave the picture symmetry, emphasis and completeness. And when its lilies turned to roses—when it blushed under the sun's first kiss—it was beautiful beyond all description. One might well say, then, "See Naples and die." The frame of the picture was charming, itself. In front, the smooth sea—a vast mosaic of many colors; the lofty islands swimming in a dreamy haze in the distance; at our end of the city the stately double peak of Vesuvius, and its strong black ribs and seams of lava stretching down to the limitless level *campagna*—a green carpet that enchants the eye and leads it on and on, past clusters of trees, and isolated houses, and snowy villages, until it shreds out in a fringe of mist and general vagueness far away. It is from the Hermitage, there on the side of Vesuvius, that one should "see Naples and die."

But do not go within the walls and look at it in detail. That takes away some of the romance of the thing. * * *

The streets are generally about wide enough for one wagon, and how they do swarm with people! It is Broadway repeated in every street, in every court, in every alley! Such masses, such throngs, such multitudes of hurrying, bustling, struggling humanity! We never saw the like of it, hardly even in New York, I think. There are seldom any sidewalks, and when there are, they are not often wide enough to pass a man on without caroming on him. So everybody walks in the street—and where the street is wide enough, carriages are forever dashing along. Why a thousand people are not run over and crippled every day is a mystery that no man can solve.

But if there is an eighth wonder in the world, it must be the dwelling-houses of Naples. I honestly believe a good majority of them are a hundred feet high! And the solid brick walls are seven feet through. You go up nine flights of stairs before you get to the "first" floor. No, not nine, but there or thereabouts. There is a little bird-cage of an iron railing in front of every window clear away up, up, up, among the eternal clouds, where the roof is, and there is always somebody looking out of every window—people of ordinary size looking out from the first floor, people a shade smaller from the second, people that look a little smaller yet from the third—and from thence upward they grow smaller and smaller by a regularly graduated diminution, till the folks in the topmost windows seem more like birds in an uncommonly tall martin-box than any thing else. The perspective of one of these narrow cracks of streets, with its rows of tall houses stretching away till they come together in the distance like railway tracks; its clothes-lines crossing over at all altitudes and waving their bannered raggedness over the swarms of people below; and the white-dressed women perched in balcony railings all the way from the pavement up to the heavens—a perspective like that is really worth going into Neapolitan details to see.

Ludwig Bemelmans
The Isle of Capri 1953

HERE IS A SIMPLE RECIPE for understanding the conformation of the island of Capri: Place on the table in front of you, to the left, a demitasse cup turned upside down; to its right, place a full-sized coffee cup, also inverted, and preferably with a chipped lip, toward you. Put a matchbox between the two cups, move the three objects close together, and drape a pale green handkerchief over the lot—and that is roughly Capri. You're looking at it now as you approach it from the north—from Naples. The small cup is Mount Tiberius (1096 feet), the large cup is Mount Solaro (1920 feet), and in the valley between, atop the matchbox, is the town of Capri. Rest a match end up on the table, leaning against the matchbox, and you have the funicular that takes you down to Marina Grande, the large port; at approximately the same spot on the other side of the island is Marina Piccola, the small port without benefit of funicular. On that side you can drape two limp strands of spaghetti, to simulate the roads that lead from Capri down to the water. Loop one piece generously for the serpentine turns—that's the one traveled by buses. Arrange the other in tight zigzags; it is the Via Krupp, a gift of the late munitions manufacturer. If you can expend two more pieces of spaghetti—a long one from Capri up to Anacapri, on the big cup, and another down to Marina Grande, you will have just about all the roads. A path leads to the top of the small cup, where the ruins of the Villa Jove are located. Like the houses of the great in Pompeii, it is restrained and simple. By comparison, for example, with Versailles, or with Mr. Hearst's San Simeon in California, it is merely a week-end bungalow. The fine pagan mood of this great ruin is marred by a badly sculptured modern Madonna planted in the middle of it, so that you cannot escape the clash of mediocre ecclesiastic art with the purity of the classic. Such clashes offend you again and again in Italy, and this is difficult to explain. For, with all the great models in front of them, and the blood of the best painters and sculptors in their veins, the Italians recently have produced very little in the way of good art.

There is the Grotta Azzura, the Blue Grotto, represented by the chipped place on the big cup; it also is decorated with an abominably executed Madonna that occupies a niche over the entrance. The roof of this tunnel is so low that you enter it sitting on the bottom of a small rowboat; even so, you have to duck while the boatman takes you in by pulling on a chain. At high tide you must lie flat in the bottom. The Blue Grotto is all that you have heard of it. The renditions of it that one finds on cheap souvenir paintings all over Capri come closest to the truth, and particularly accurate is the light effect on the top and the sidewalls. The local artists treat it as if they were showing a cavern with luminous, bluish worms crawling up the walls and across the vaulted ceiling.

On top of the smaller of the two coffee cups, on a rocky promontory that rises above Capri, is a villa with a sweeping view of the Mediterranean on both sides of the island. It is owned by Gaetano Parente, who has the long legs necessary to negotiate several times a day the two-hundred-odd stone steps by which the villa is reached. He is never without a small dog, a breed peculiar to the island and, like its population, of the most varied nomenclature.

"Without inflicting on you the tyranny of dates and too many names," said Gaetano Parente, "I will give you the briefest kind of history of Capri." We were walking down the Via Krupp. That is, he was walking—I ran.

"Almost everyone who has written a book here has taken something from a volume called *Ricerche Storiche sull' Isola di Capri*, by Rosario Mangoni. I recommend it to you, and also one called *The Book of Capri*, by Harold E. Trower, onetime British consul here. One cannot write about Italy without quoting from one book or another, or from inscriptions on ancient metals, stones, wood, canvases, or tapestries, that are in evidence everywhere.

"The story goes something like this: The Emperor Augustus saw Capri's possibilities, and it was he, not Tiberius, who built it up. Tiberius came later and improved it, making of it for a while a rest place and camp for soldiers of the Roman Empire. His name is more in evidence here today than that of Augustus.

"After Tiberius, Capri for a few hundred years was left in solitude. I'll spare you history here, and we will move up to when it was rediscovered as a pleasure place, by Germans, who at the time headed a spiritual back-to-nature movement. They came here, shouted, '*Wunderbar,*' and walked about naked, carrying their children on both shoulders. They lived on fruit and vegetables, picked wildflowers, and named butterflies that until then had never been properly catalogued.

"After these blond nudists the English arrived—the Oxford boys, the Shelley and Keats group—and they were very impressed by the fine physiques of the native fishermen. Those romantic boys did a lot for Capri, constantly singing its praises. They never tired of adoring this happy, brown people, and strangely enough, the propaganda brought on a great horde of British spinsters. There was no harbor then, and the ladies were carried ashore in the strong arms of the picturesque natives. Then came other English breeds, noblemen, industrialists, and archæologists, who bought the best statuary and shipped it to the British Museum.

"Now Capri was really famous. The kings came, and the Russian grand dukes; the Kaiser visited on his yacht. All the world came—the old rich, the *nouveaux riches*, and tycoons like Krupp and Axel Wenner-Gren; also Lenin, and even Trotsky. Today an American woman, Mrs. Harrison Williams, is the Queen of the Isle. Of Italians, we have relatively few that are villa owners.

"Of all the things that have gone on here you find the remnants not only in the earth but also in the faces about you. Giovanni is a fisherman at Marina Grande—his face is out of the senate chambers of Rome in the time of Augustus. Put a toga on the fat chauffeur that drives the Anacapri bus, and you have Nero. Look at the man coming out of the Restaurant Hidigeigei every day after lunch; he wears his beard like Franz Josef of Hapsburg and looks like him. It's all preserved here as in an album, including some of the English, who still adore the native fishermen. The English spinsters are fewer now on account of travel restrictions, but instead we have the Americans, who outdo everyone else in letting their hair down and admiring everything, especially a few women hair-let-downers, who admire the fishermen even more violently than do the English boys."

John Gibbons
All the Gloating I Wanted 1932

IT IS IN ITS WAY A BIT LIKE going into the London Zoo. There is a line of turnstiles and ticket-offices, and you pay so many *lire* to the Italian Ministry of Instruction and pass through the clicking gates. And once you are inside you are besieged by a crowd of touts all speaking scraps of every language and all anxious to take you round. And besides them there are other men with umbrellaed and awned wheel-chairs, rather like those we had at Wembley, and they want the job of dragging you round the sights. For Pompeii in A.D. 79 was very nearly a thirty-thousand population town, so it is quite a big place, and stretches quite a long way under that perfectly scorching sun. But you need not hire anybody at all for as there are notices in every language all round to tell you, the Government has its own official uniformed guides there, and they neither need nor are supposed to take any tips. I, of course, went alone, but though I did not have a guide I was very interested in the man who followed me for the first few yards, for he kept telling me about the sights that he would show me. "There are some things," he said leeringly, "that are for the ladies, and there are other things that are for the gentlemen." Somehow it sounded like a bit out of Holy Writ.

I knew, of course, what he meant: the place that used to be a Gay House, and there are some beastly paintings on the wall which have lasted all down the centuries. Quite famous it is, and even I had heard of it. There are nasty old gentlemen, I believe, who pay quite a lot of good money for copies of the frescoes, so that in their leisure hours they may have something to gloat over. As a matter of fact, I went to the place, and then did not go inside. It is down a lane that is in every sense shady, and you might as well sit somewhere out of that awful sun. I could get all the gloating I personally wanted out of the other people who did go there and who went inside. I took quite a little census of them in the half-hour or so I sat there.

Our own English gentlemen came easily first. You could always pick them out as they furtively rounded the corner of the lane. Because they all had exactly the same expression. "Bless my soul! I never meant to come here, but now that accident has brought me I suppose I might as well go through with it. Only I do hope that nobody in Ealing gets to hear about it." The Germans now were quite different, with a frank licking of the lips at the sensual treat in store. At least they did not pretend at all that they were there by accident. And the Latins were different again, in entirely another way. For if they came down the lane at all they generally did not take the trouble to go inside. And if they did go, they went perfectly naturally and without the faintest self-consciousness. I watched a party of French—for there are not so many Italians in Pompeii—and the men said something to their wives, and then with a laugh passed inside the place. And the women stopped outside with a little shrug at masculine weakness and the precise air with which two English girls might have let their menfolk off the chain for a minute to go and have a glass of bitter. They did not want one themselves—but men will be men, poor things!

But the funniest of all was an American. For it was a woman, and she knew what was inside and wanted to go simply as a matter of sex right. "Why," she put it to the quite uncomprehending Italian official, "should she not see what any man was allowed to see? She had paid at the gates like any man, and was not her money just as good as a man's?" But the Italian was not argumentative. He had his orders. Any man, no woman. And the American feminist did not get in.

Mr Punch
The New Michelin Guide
to Mafia Sicily 1983

N RECENT MONTHS THE KILLINGS in Sicily have reached new dimensions. In one week eleven people were rubbed out in less time than it takes to cook *spaghetti vongole*.

A growing trend appears to be for *mafiosi* to be killed while they are out eating in restaurants, where they are relaxed and vulnerable. Indeed, so strong is this practice that the publishers of the Michelin travel guides have decided to bring out a special Sicilian edition in which the pictorial code they use has been amended in a number of vital ways to take in the particular flavour of Sicilian life.

✿	Complimentary flowers at your funeral.
✿✿	Flowers, plus full Mafia military honours.
✿✿✿	Flowers, honours, plus one stolen Old Master sent to your next of kin.
🏛	Cemetery with mausoleum.
🏛	Cemetery without mausoleum.
♿	Beware kneecappings.
〰	Number of drownings reported at time of going to press.
🏚	"Psycho" method sometimes used in this establishment.
🐕	Only dogs killed so far.
✗ ✗ ✗ ✗	Stabbings a speciality.
🚗	Ambulance on premises.
🚗	Hearse on premises.

P	Priest on premises.
☎	Phones tapped by the Godfather.
☎	Phones tapped by the police.
🚶	*Omertà* operates—i.e., keep your mouth shut if you see anything— well, *unusual*.
0437	Local number for the Samaritans.
⚑ 18	Godfather's handicap; unwise to play better.
🐎	Do not expect meals here to be cheap. You will be taken for a ride.
A6	*Allettamento enorme*. Literally translated, this old Sicilian phrase means "enormous bribe". Generally given to the *maitre d'* before the main course. Don't leave home without it.
🪑	Old people sighted; worth a detour.

J. Ross Browne
The Catacombs of Palermo 1855

CHIEF AMONG THE WONDERS of Palermo are the Catacombs of the Capuchin Convent, near the Porta d'Ossuna. It is said to be a place of great antiquity; many of the bodies have been preserved in it for centuries, and still retain much of their original freshness. Entering the ancient and ruinous court of the convent, distant about a mile from the city, I was conducted by a ghostly-looking monk through some dark passages to the subterranean apartments of the dead. It was not my first visit to a place of this kind, but I must confess the sight was rather startling. It was like a revel of the dead—a horrible, grinning, ghastly exhibition of skeleton forms, sightless eyes, and shining teeth, jaws distended, and bony hands outstretched; heads without bodies, and bodies without heads—the young, the old, the brave, the once beautiful and gay, all mingled in the ghastly throng. I walked through long subterranean passages, lined with the dead on both sides; with a stealthy and measured tread I stepped, for they seemed to stare at the intrusion, and their skeleton fingers vibrated as if yearning to grasp the living in their embrace. Long rows of upright niches are cut into the walls on each side; in every niche a skeleton form stands erect as in life, habited in a robe of black; the face, hands, and feet naked, withered, and of an ashy hue; the grizzled beards still hanging in tufts from the jaws, and in the recent cases the hair still clinging to the skull, but matted and dry. To each corpse is attached a label upon which is written the name and the date of decease, and a cross or the image of the Saviour.

Soon recovering from the shock of the first impression, I was struck with the wonderful variety and marked expression of character in the faces and forms around me. There were progressive dates of death, extending from remote centuries up to the present period, the niches being so arranged as to admit of a regular order of deposit. Many of the bodies stood erect, as if just lifted from the death-bed; the faces colorless, and the horrible agonies of dissolution stamped upon the features; the lower jaws hanging upon the breast; the teeth grinning and glistening between the parched lips, and the black hue of sickness about the mouth and around the sunken sockets of the eyes; and in some the sightless orbs were open and staring with a wild glare of affright, as if peering into the awful mysteries of the future; while others wore a grotesque laugh of derision still more appalling, with the muscles of the mouth drawn up, the eyebrows lifted, the head tilted knowingly on one side, the hair matted in horny tufts, the bare spots on the skulls, like the piebald wig of a harlequin; the skeleton arms outstretched, and the bony fingers spread as if to clutch the relentless destroyer, and wrestle with him to the last. These I fancied were lively fellows, who were carried off suddenly after a midnight carouse. I sat down on a box containing a dead child, and looked up at a row of bodies opposite that attracted my notice in a particular degree. In the middle stood a rolicking fellow, about two years dead, whose sunken eyes appeared still to burn with the fire of life and humor. His hands were lifted in a deprecating manner over a congregation of corpses sitting on a shelf below. Some appeared to be listening; some grinning at his humorous harangue; others, with their heads together, seemed to question the propriety of his anecdotes; old gentlemen, with knitted brows and lantern jaws; ranges of bodies stood on each side of him as if laughing, talking, praying, dying, suffering, listening, rejoicing, and feasting at the banquet of death. One little man, in a dingy suit of black, sat in a corner; the end of his nose was eaten off by the worms; his mouth was compressed, and had a pinched expression; his hands grasped eagerly at something. I thought that little man was a miser, whose death was caused by starvation. Another figure, a large portly body, stood in a conspicuous part of the vault; it was the corpse of a fat old bishop, whose jaws were still rotund and smooth with good living, and his sleek hair was patted down to his head as with the oil of bygone roast beefs and macaroni soups, and his jolly cast of countenance betokened a system liberally supplied with the juices of life, and a conscience rendered easy by attention to the creature comforts. That man lived an easy life, and died of good feeding.

*"When in Rome do as the Romans do?
My God! They don't do anything."*

PEOPLE

❧Italians

❧*We decided to save the best part of Italy for last: its
people. If Italy didn't have a single art treasure, a single
strand of spaghettini, a single automobile accident, it
would still have Italianos. You can say what you want
about Italians, but no one can name another people that
are so much themselves. Whether they are guiding you,
serving you dinner, or simply talking together, wherever
you go there they are, in every museum and restaurant, at
every hotel and ruin, on every mountain, river, and lake,
welcoming, quarreling, insisting, or just being bureau-
cratic in their very special way.*

*Since the Italians are such a fertile subject for humor
(please do not think any double entendre was intended),
we have an unusually superb lineup of witnesses to tell
you what they've seen.*

*Besides sporty cars, leather, and all those doo-dads,
the Italians are unsurpassed in manufacturing noise. One
would think that their tendency to gesticulate would damp-
en the enthusiasm of their speech and other accompani-
ments, but just as a runner's rhythmic arm movements
make him run all the faster, the Italian's arhythmic body
movements make him talk all the louder. Art Buchwald
analyzes the broader form of the activity, or sport as he
prefers to call it, that is, noisemaking in general. Then
humorist Irvin S. Cobb and travel writers Anne Hol-
lingsworth Wharton and Aubrey Menen provide us with
studies of the art of Italian conversation, and tips on how
to enjoy or, at least, survive it.*

159

Art Buchwald
The National Italian Sport 1960

THE SITE FOR THIS YEAR'S summer Olympics is Rome. The Italians are great sports lovers, and the national sport of Italy is *Far Rumore* (translation—"to make noise"). The sport originated some time in the Middle Ages in Sicily when it was discovered that visitors to the island were sleeping instead of buying souvenirs in the shops.

This infuriated the Sicilian merchants so much that they hired men and women to stand under the windows of tourists and shout at each other.

Later on they hired pig beaters and donkey-cart owners to drive around the main streets at three and four in the morning. The screaming of the pigs and the rattling of the carts drove the visitors out into the streets, where they had nothing else to do but shop. The Sicilian merchants prospered, and the idea soon caught on on the mainland.

Today there isn't a town in Italy that doesn't have several first-class *Far Rumore* teams. While refinements have been added, the objective of the sport is still the same—to keep tourists from sleeping.

In some cities, motor scooters and Ferraris have replaced the pigs and donkey carts, and the automobile horn is as important to the *Far Rumore* player as the cape is to the matador.

Roger Price, who was recently in Naples, reports he was there for the regional tryouts, which were held in front of his window at the Hotel Excelsior. The people around Naples, he said, shun modern methods and prefer to holler.

"The champion hollerer of Naples had died since the previous tryouts," Mr. Price told me, "and so they held a minute of noise for him.

"Then they got on with the games. The tryouts are always held between midnight and eight in the morning. There are different categories. But the results are always the same. The one who wakes up the most tourists, wins.

"There are the singles matches, when each participant must holler alone. Then there are the mixed doubles, when husbands and wives compete against each other. Finally there are the team matches, in which teams composed of men who have consumed a bottle of wine apiece start shouting at each other.

"The teams are cheered on by spectators, and there is always a great deal of arguing after the matches about who made the most noise, the teams or the spectators."

In Rome the mixed doubles are held between teams of sports cars and motor scooters on the Via Veneto. The mufflers are taken off the vehicles exactly at midnight, and the contest goes on until dawn. It isn't necessary for the vehicle to move; as long as their motors are running they are in the game.

As you go farther north, *Far Rumore* takes on a different flavor. In Florence William Dana, an American tourist, reports, *Far Rumore* is played with garbage pails, and the teams are made up of the building superintendents on one hand and the garbage collectors on the other. For years, the building superintendents won the contest, but recently the garbage collectors have been winning, thanks to a new coach named Giuseppe Casaldiavolo. The coach invented the famed "Casaldiavolo pass," in which the garbage pail is slammed against the side of the truck before the garbage is emptied. Since then the tourists have given the nod to the collectors, and the superintendents are looking around for a new coach.

In Venice *Far Rumore* is played between the gondoliers and the motorboats. The gondoliers used to sing to keep tourists awake, but in recent times, every time they started, the motorboat owners revved up their engines and drowned them out.

This so infuriated the gondoliers that they brought in a team of hollerers from Naples, and now, instead of singing, the gondoliers holler oaths at the motorboats. Since then the matches have been even.

Even in the smaller towns *Far Rumore* is played. Mr. Price reports he was in a small town near Genoa, where, instead of hollering or racing their motors, the peasants played by banging a stick against his car.

The world record for a tourist sleeping in Italy is three hours and forty-seven minutes. It's held by a ninety-year-old Frenchman named Alain Bernheim, who lost his hearing aid an hour before he went to sleep, and the motor scooter assigned to his window ran out of gas.

Irvin S. Cobb
The Art of Conversation 1913

THE AVERAGE AMERICAN, on the eve of going to Europe, thinks of the European as speaking each his own language. He conceives of the Poles speaking Polar; of the Hollanders talking Hollandaise; of the Swiss as employing Schweitzer for ordinary conversations and yodeling when addressing friends at a distance; and so on. Such, however, is rarely the case. Nearly every person with whom one comes in contact in Europe appears to have fluent command of several tongues besides his or her own. It is true this does not apply to Italy, where the natives mainly stick to Italian; but then, Italian is not a language. It is a calisthenic.

Between Rome and Florence, our train stopped at a small way station in the mountains. As soon as the little locomotive had panted itself to a standstill the train hands, following their habit, piled off the cars and engaged in a tremendous confab with the assembled officials on the platform. Immediately all the loafers in sight drew cards. A drowsy hillsman, muffled to his back hair in a long brown cloak, and with buskins on his legs such as a stage bandit wears, was dozing against the wall. He looked as though he had stepped right out of a comic opera to add picturesqueness to the scene. He roused himself and joined in; so did a bearded party who, to judge by his uniform, was either a Knight of Pythias or a general in the army; so did all the rest of the crowd. In ten seconds they were jammed together in a hard knot, and going it on the high speed with the muffler off, fine white teeth shining, arms flying, shoulders shrugging, spinal columns writhing, mustaches rising and falling, legs wriggling, scalps and ears following suit. Feeding hour in the parrot cage at the zoo never produced anything like so noisy and animated a scene. In these parts acute hysteria is not a symptom; it is merely a state of mind.

A waiter in soiled habiliments hurried up, abandoning chances of trade at the prospect of something infinitely more exciting. He wanted to stick his oar into the argument. He had a few pregnant thoughts of his own craving utterance, you could tell that. But he was handicapped into a state of dumbness by the fact that he needed both arms to balance a tray of wine and sandwiches on his head. Merely using his voice in that company would not have counted. He stood it as long as he could, which was not very long, let me tell you. Then he slammed his tray down on the platform and, with one quick movement, jerked his coat sleeves back to his elbows, and inside thirty seconds he had the floor in both hands, as it were. He conversed mainly with the Australian crawl stroke, but once in a while switched to the Spencerian free-arm movement and occasionally introduced the Chautauqua salute with telling effect.

Anne Hollingsworth Wharton
Interpreting a Quarrel 1906

TURNING A CORNER, we suddenly found ourselves in the midst of a quarrel, or a violent altercation at the best, between a pretty *signora* at a fourth-floor window and a vendor of fruits and vegetables on the sidewalk below. The language which the lady used, as she leaned far out of the window, was so vigorous that no interpreter was needed to make her meaning plain; the merchant was a charlatan and a villain; the saints were all called upon as witnesses to his depravity. He, the so-called vendor of over-ripe fruit, pointed to his wares, beating his breast and spreading out his hands in token of his spotless innocence. He sell over-ripe oranges? All his neighbors would testify to his poverty and that of his family because he, honest one, daily sacrificed hundreds of oranges to satisfy his unreasonable customers!

The *signora*'s dark eyes flashed, the Spanish *mantilla* upon her head shook in sympathy with the violence of her emotions, as she repeated her vocabulary of epithets. We were thankful that four stories separated the combatants, and retiring under the shadow of a doorway we anxiously awaited results. Something happened, we know not what; the fruit may have been reduced the fraction of a penny; whatever it was, a truce was declared, during which the *signora*'s basket, filled with fruit and artichokes, was drawn up to the window by a rope. After the lady had carefully inspected each individual fruit and vegetable, she smiled blandly, lowered some money in her basket, and the pair parted with bows and compliments. Juliet on her balcony could not have been more graceful, nor Romeo on the pavement below more gallant than this shabby *venditore*, as he swept the ground with his cap, one hand upon his heart!

Feeling that we owed something to somebody for the pleasure that this little drama had afforded us, we crossed the street and bought from the chief actor some fresh dates such as we had first tasted in Algiers. As we paid the asking price without protest, we felt quite sure that the valiant little merchant was making off us anything that he may have lost in his previous transaction; but the dates, of a delicate amber color, as sweet as honey and almost as transparent, were worth whatever price we paid for them.

Aubrey Menen
Irony As an Instrument 1962

WE ALL KNOW THAT ITALIAN is the best language to sing in. But that is because it has been sung for centuries, not only to music, but every time that Italians use it to talk with. The intonations have been elaborated so much that an Italian can say a sentence ten different ways and give it as many different meanings. I remember that when I felt that I had mastered Italian, I rather vaingloriously asked a Roman professor of languages to tell me what faults still remained. He was most reluctant to do so but when I pressed him, he said, "My dear sir, your Italian is remarkably correct, but unfortunately it is at the same time all wrong. I do not suppose anybody has told you this—we rarely tell foreigners—but we speak our language as a form of artistic expression. You speak Italian as you speak English: you use it to communicate your ideas. We do speak that way sometimes, but only on the long-distance telephone, which is rather expensive here in Italy. When we speak face to face, we are less concerned in exchanging ideas than in expressing the richness of our own creative gifts. We listen to the other person but we listen much more to ourselves. When I am addressed by a foreigner, I feel I am back doing my military service and listening to my sergeant putting our company into the picture for an exercise." Having had my ears thus politely boxed, I began to listen with them and I found, of course, that what he said was true.

I also discovered something that should be of interest to every foreign visitor. The Italians delight in being rude to foreigners in such a manner that the foreigner never knows it. The instrument they use is irony, and that can go right through a stranger and come out on the other side without leaving a mark. Foreigners are always impressed by the compliments that are heaped on them in Italy—about their knowledge of the language, the beauty of their children, the excellence of their motorcars. But compliments are paid in two ways. The first is, to use the Italian phrase, "from the heart," which does not mean a warm gush of emotion. It means that it is paid with every possible richness of inflection, with emphasis on key words and with a variety of grace notes in all the vowels. This is the compliment the Italians really mean. The other, which they do not, is said with decision, as though it is something everybody knows. The emphasis is light, the vowel sounds sober, and the voice is soft. "But, of course, Mrs. Smith, your children are beautifully behaved. Who could think otherwise?" Mrs. Smith has been skewered. Her children are brats.

But the most striking thing of all is that an Italian, even when he is thoroughly angry, will not say anything which offends his sense of euphony of the language. One car, for example, bumps into another. The two owners leap out of their seats and meet in the street. A crowd gathers. The resulting altercation seems to the foreigner comically loquacious. But an Italian cannot begin a conversation with, "Damn your eyes, you blithering idiot." He does not swear. If he does, he can be arrested. He may not, in fact, call the other man a cretin. An American friend of mine was fined for using the word. It was thought indecorous.

Instead, the drivers must begin and continue euphonious-ly. That is why the altercation commences with an exchange of highly sarcastic compliments. "And you, sir, you undoubtedly are a General of the Carabinieri on an urgent national mission to permit yourself to drive on the wrong side of the road in flagrant contravention of the Highway Code, which, with a powerful car like that, you certainly know backwards." "And you, sir, driving at that pace are no doubt a doctor urgently summoned to the Pope's bedside." And so on. It is the lovely sound which counts and it is this that the crowd is listening to.

Foreign customs can get rather confusing, and Italian ones, no matter how familiar we think they are from all the films we've seen—in fact because of this apparent familiarity—are as confusing as any. Our next selection is a story by the excellent American storyteller Francis Steegmuller, and then English poet Donald Hall tells us the origin of a local fair and Mark Twain casts light on the ultimate Italian experience: the miracle.

Francis Steegmuller
Ciao Fabrizio 1964

THE FISHING VILLAGE called—let us say—Matrani is on the Italian coast near Amalfi. I recently visited a friend who lives there, and found it a quiet place most of the week, because that was off season. Weekends it was lively. Families from Naples, who owned villas on the nearby slopes, poured into the village, with their guests and their cars, creating an air of carnival—the air, my friend told me, that characterized the place during the months of July and August. During those months, not only did the Neapolitans occupy their villas continuously, but vacationers, both Italian and foreign, crowded the hotels and beaches, and Matrani briefly became a second Capri.

As it was, during the several weeks of my visit the dining terrace of Matrani's best restaurant, La Torre dei Saraceni, was an amusing spot on Friday and Saturday nights. Tables were reserved, and at about nine o'clock the Neapolitans began to arrive—a handsome, decorative set. The ladies, elaborately hairdressed and bejeweled, wore evening gowns that were usually very bright and cut low, and they carried all kinds of scarves and stoles, from chiffon to mink, against the Mediterranean night breeze. The men favored sport shirts, foulards, and cashmere sweaters, above immaculate pastel-colored slacks. Everybody seemed to know everybody. Tables were often placed end to end in advance and decorated with garlands of rambler roses and bougainvillea to await the arrival of a large party coming from a "cocktail" in one or another of the villas; or two or more tables would be pushed together impromptu as groups, arriving separately, coalesced with shrill cries of surprise. I seldom heard an introduction performed. Once in a while, an Ingegnere So-and-So and his wife—who usually seemed to come from Milan—would be presented by their hostess to her fellow Marchese and Contesse and to the assorted gentlemen, but in general the people who came to the terrace were like an enormous lot of cousins transplanted in a body from adjoining Neapolitan town houses to similarly adjacent villas on a single enclosed estate.

One Friday night at the Torre dei Saraceni, my friend and I found ourselves seated close to a particularly long row of tables set for at least twenty persons and strewn not with the usual garden flowers but with dozens of long-stemmed roses, all of the same beautiful variety often seen around Naples—creamy yellow petals edged with crimson. *"Uno sposalizio napoletano"*—a Neapolitan wedding—our waiter told us, and we looked forward to seeing some of the usual weekend habitués gathered together to celebrate this further solidifying of their clan. But when the wedding company arrived, quite late, after all other tables were occupied, they were people we had never seen before except for one, known to my friend as the mayor of Matrani. More formally dressed—the men in dark city suits, and some of the older ladies even wearing hats—they had the same air of high fashion as the rest, and, indeed, during the flurry of seating quite a number of people came over from other tables to shake the hands of the happy pair and of the two older couples who were obviously their parents. The visitors would murmur congratulations—we were struck by a marked softening of their Neapolitan voices, during these moments, as contrasted with the rather strident gaiety they displayed among themselves—and would then return to their own tables. Clearly, the members of this wedding party were *per bene*—known and accepted by the titled crowd from the villas—but also they seemed to be in a curious isolation, self-sufficient and enclosed.

Not that there wasn't some gaiety at the wedding table. The bride's eyes were red, and her mother's eyes, too—one expects a few red eyes at a wedding—but a half-dozen or so adorable small children, who, we guessed, must have been flower girls and pages at the ceremony, kept jumping down from their chairs and moving happily about the table, getting in the way of the waiters and receiving not scoldings but kisses from their elders. And among the guests farthest from the immediate bridal party there was plenty of smiling, gesturing, and calling back and forth.

However, the bride was certainly overwrought. She was a beautiful ash-blonde girl, tall, with a splendid carriage and a classic profile, wearing a low-cut café-au-lait taffeta dress. From time to time, she would dab at her eyes with her handkerchief, and at one point she laid her head on the shoulder of her father, next to whom she sat, and held her handkerchief to her eyes as he caressed her and murmured into her ear. The groom seemed to pay no attention to this. He was a small, mean-looking fellow, lacking even the kind of distinction that his tailor had given his suit, the jacket of which was startlingly wasp-waisted and slashed with exaggerated side vents. The widespread white points of his shirt collar emphasized the pinched, almost scrawny quality of his features and the lumpiness of his Adam's apple. He was young, but there was nothing about him that seemed so; he was like an ageless little clerk. He kept up a grave, unsmiling conversation with his parents—the three of them formed a unit within a unit—and he seemed to have a connection with his beautiful bride only when they stood up together to receive someone's congratulations. At one point, the bride's mother rose abruptly and beckoned to two young women of the party, who were perhaps the bridesmaids. They went to the bride, who rose also, and the four of them left the terrace in a cluster. As they passed us, the bride kept her face averted, but we could hear her sob, and when they returned, after what must have been consolation and repair in the ladies' room, her eyes and her mother's were still red. The bridegroom still seemed unconcerned. Nor did any of the Neapolitans at the other tables react to this evident distress. We wondered whether good manners made them pretend to be unaware, or whether to them everything seemed normal.

Meanwhile, on the harborside promenade just under the restaurant terrace where we were sitting, a crowd had been gathering—a larger crowd than the one on most pleasant weekend nights, when the Matranesi and *paesani* from neighboring villages thronged the pavement along the little fishing port until midnight. There was an air of expectancy, and, indeed, our waiter most exceptionally brought us our bill before we asked for it and urged us not to lose any time. "Signori," he said, "the fireworks will begin very soon now, and you'll want to find a good place. The best view will be from the other side of the harbor, and it will take you a little time to push through the crowd." He pointed to the beach, and, through the darkness, we saw that a sort of framework had been erected and that dim figures were putting finishing touches to what looked like improvised rocket-launching pads. After lingering less long than usual over our coffee, we paid and left. The wedding party was drinking champagne. There were raised glasses and exchanges of greetings, but no speeches or toasts. The ladies were fussing with their handbags; the dinner was ending.

The quay on the far side of the harbor was crowded when we got there, everyone much interested in the half-dozen smartly varnished motor launches that were floating at the foot of the water steps leading down from the mole. Their boatmen, in caps and striped jerseys, were waiting at the wheels, and three or four local fishermen were on duty at the ropes. People in the crowd were telling each other that the craft had been hired in Amalfi—there was nothing to compare with them for rent in poor Matrani. From here, the fireworks installation on the beach could be seen more clearly; the tilted rocket platforms, and the larger contraption that looked like the skeleton for a big roadside billboard.

Then came the wedding party, a procession more or less in irregular double file, advancing along the waterfront from the Torre dei Saraceni. The bride now carried a pale mink stole. The mayor of Matrani was walking ahead of her, motioning importantly to the spectators to make way, and back and forth along the line of march strode the two local *carabinieri*, occasionally stretching out their arms as symbolic fences. With a series of roars, the motors of the hired launches sprang to life, a fisherman held the first one close to the quay with a boat hook, and after a little flurry over precedence the wedding party began to embark. As each boat filled, it drew away and waited a dozen yards offshore, and when the last boatload took off, all the motors roared in unison, and the entire flotilla took off into the night. The crowd, which had been murmuring in admiration of the fine clothes and lovely women and general elegance of the party, now burst into cheers and shouts: *"Buon viaggio!" "Auguri!" "Addio!" "Ciao!"*

Where was the party off to, in its hired craft? Were they all returning by water to Naples? Would they split up, the bride and groom going perhaps to honeymoon on Capri, only a few miles away? But the bride and groom had not stepped alone into their launch; their two sets of parents had embarked with them. Maybe they were all just going to Amalfi, where the boats had come from, and where hired limousines or their own cars would take them to different destinations. Considering what my friend and I learned later about this wedding party, there must have been plenty of people in the crowd there on the quay who knew its destination and all the facts concerning it. But in Matrani gossip and speculation are infinitely more fun than accurate statement, and all we heard around us was questions and various guesses. Everybody did know one thing: as soon as the boats were far enough offshore to get the full effect, the fireworks would begin. And scarcely had the last chug of a motor died away when the first illumination burst out. It was the big framework, the set piece, and after some preliminary spluttering and fizzing it revealed itself as truly a great, glowing signboard. In tow lines of glittering live letters it proclaimed its message:

CIAO ADRIANA
CIAO FABRIZIO

"Com'è bello!" "Bellissimo!" "O!" "Guarda!" the exclamations sprang from the delighted crowd. And then the rockets began. Roman candles, sprays, baskets of flowers—the whole gamut of a fireworks display flung

itself into the darkness and out over the Mediterranean. Explosions, rumbles, and swishes vied with human shrieks. The air filled with sulphur, and we saw isolated balls of incandescence swerve from their course and strike the hillsides that half enclosed the port and—for we had been having a drought in Matrani—setting fire to plots of grass and, for all we knew, to houses, or to pieces of the laundry that is perpetually hanging on clotheslines on Matrani terraces.

On and on went the display, and on the upper slopes patches of flame kept appearing, only to be doused by watchful householders, who, being true Matranesi, probably did not mind a little charring in return for the fun. Long before the show was over, my friend and I climbed up the steep streets to his house. From his balcony, we saw it end at last in a tremendous aerial bouquet of assorted colors and numerous booms, and, down on the beach—well timed to end with the rest—the gradual fading out of

CIAO ADRIANA
CIAO FABRIZIO

Toward noon the next day, Maria, my friend's cook, arrived as usual with a full market basket, ready to make lunch. "Well," she said, "this has been an unusual morning. I've done something I don't do every day. I've been to a wedding."

"You have?" my friend said. "We almost went to one last night. At least, we saw the end of one, and you must have, too. How did you like the fireworks?"

Maria stared at us. "You say you saw the end of a wedding last night?" she said slowly. We were all talking Italian, but for a moment she acted as though my friend's words had been uttered in some strange tongue that she had to take time to translate. "What did you see?"

We told her about the *sposalizio* dinner at the Torre dei Saraceni, and the departure of the party. "You must have been watching at least the rest of it from somewhere yourself," my friend said. "Certainly you saw the big illuminated sign wishing luck to the bride and groom?"

Maria shook her head. She began a movement of her right hand that looked suspiciously like the start of a sign of the Cross, then stopped it, probably out of courtesy. "You Americans have the strangest ideas about things," she said, gravely. "No wonder we sometimes ask ourselves whether you are *cristiani*. You obviously understood nothing about what took place last night. Nothing. For one thing, who ever heard of an evening banquet *following* a Christian wedding? The real wedding banquet of those people you saw last night is about to take place now—*now*, at any moment, at the Torre dei Saraceni. And besides—"

"But the waiter told us it was a *sposalizio*," my friend said. "And there was that sign—"

"Momento," said Maria. *"Prego."* She held up her hand.

If Maria is a privileged character in my friend's house, it is because she is an extraordinary one. A native of Matrani, untraveled beyond Naples except for one great weekend excursion with a group of pilgrims to St. Peter's in Rome, where she saw the Pope, and only fairly literate, she nonetheless possesses an unusual ability to see events in larger contexts. It was a larger context that she proceeded to sketch for us now, after characteristically asking our permission to do so: *"Permettono, signori, che racconti una storia?"*

"Dica," said my friend.

And Maria began. "A few years ago in Naples," she said, "when they were widening a street, they came on a big underground cemetery"—*una catacomba,* she called it, *un ossario piuttosto, molto antico*—"that nobody knew was there. It was full of skulls and bones, all neatly arranged on shelves cut out of the rock. The engineers were going to clear it out, do away with it, but the people of the neighborhood were furious, and staged a real war. It was their cemetery, they said, even if they'd never known anything about it, and they wanted to keep it. They just invaded the place and refused to budge. The women were especially fierce, but plenty of men joined in, and they defended their cemetery like a fortress, and wouldn't let the workmen touch a thing. They won, too. The engineers gave in. They begged to be allowed to straighten the place a little, saying it really wasn't sanitary, but the citizens said we'll do it ourselves, thank you, just leave us alone. So the engineers built a nice entrance and a door—you can see it any time; it looks like one of the entrances to the Naples subway, the Metropolitana, only smaller—and the neighborhood people did do a wonderful job of making the place neat, rearranging bones that had fallen down over the centuries, and sweeping out the corridors.

"And they set up a kind of lottery in the neighborhood, and, according to the number you picked, you could choose your skull. They were most interested in the skulls, of course, they being more human than the rest of the bones. Each person, you might say, *adopted* the skull he or she chose, and sometimes gave it a name, and some people put glass bells over their skulls with labels on them to keep them private and free from dust. The people go down there and talk to them, and say their prayers in front of them. It's a real curiosity, that cemetery—one of the sights of Naples.

"I went to see it once. One of my cousins told me I shouldn't miss it. And the first thing I saw, that morning down there, was a woman of the neighborhood kneeling on a little cushion she'd brought with her, talking to her skull. The glass bell that had been over it was all moist on the inside, and the woman had taken it off and was drying it with her handkerchief. 'Poor little thing,' she was saying to the skull, 'how you did sweat during the night! We must think of some way to keep you dry. The night sweat is unhealthy, my darling, but never fear, your Concetta will take care of you. Have faith in your Concetta.' And then she began to say an Ave Maria. Up and down the corridors were other women, and men, too, kneeling on cushions in front of their skulls and murmuring to them. I said to my cousin, 'These skulls are so ancient—aren't they the skulls of *pagani?*' And my cousin said, '*Pagani* or *cristiani*, what's the difference? They're all *morti*, and the *morti* all deserve our prayers and love, because they were once just like us.'"

Maria looked at us. It was clear from her look that she had made a point—one that we should have got, or begun to get. But she is a kindly soul, and, quickly deciding, apparently, that clear though her point was to *her*, we might be forgiven for still remaining in the dark, she went on almost at once. "Neapolitans do more than just respect the dead, Signori," she said. "They love them, and they have many ways of inviting them to go on living with them. That cemetery my cousin took me to is just one example. There was another example in that dinner and fireworks last night, and in the wedding this morning. Did you really think that the name Fabrizio on the fireworks sign was the name of the bridegroom?"

She stopped to enjoy our astonishment.

"Didn't you see how insignificant that little bridegroom was?" she went on. "He's a *barone*, but that doesn't mean much in Naples. Don't you know the story of how one of the old kings of Naples created a hundred or so *baroni* at one sweep, without meaning to? Some tradesmen called on him in a body, at the crack of dawn one morning, with a petition, and they made so much noise in the anteroom that they woke him up. He came out, rubbing his eyes. 'Good morning, *baroni*,' he said sarcastically. 'Thanks for putting me at the top of your list of things to do today.' That was enough for them. They forgot their petition, and every one of them and their descendants called himself *barone* ever after. I think the little *barone* bridegroom must be that kind of a nobleman.

"No, most titles are worth only one thing to a man in Naples—a little money if somebody wants to buy you for his daughter. That's the case in the present instance. The bride's family is very rich. During the war, they left Naples to escape the bombing, and came to Matrani. There were four of them then. The bride was a little girl, of course, and she had a brother a few years older, named Fabrizio. He was killed, here in Matrani, when an army truck ran over him. He was buried in the cemetery here. Later, the rest returned to Naples, but they come every year to visit his grave, and, being Neapolitans, they naturally wanted him to participate in his sister's wedding. So they came to Matrani to celebrate it. They have no villa here, so they hired a lot of hotel rooms for themselves and their guests, and last night they had the prewedding dinner and the fireworks that included Fabrizio. Naturally, the bride was upset, thinking of her brother all the time. She adored him when she was a little girl."

"Where did they go off to in the boats?" my friend asked.

"Only offshore, toward Capri, to look back and see the fireworks," said Maria. "They returned to port after the display was over, and spent the night in their various hotels. By the way, the bride's father is going to have at least one lawsuit on his hands, or anyway a settlement. Donna Teresa, up on the north cliff, wasn't home last night, and when she got back this morning she found a patch of her vineyard burned to cinders by a rocket. Donna Teresa loves her grapes, and she'll expect to be paid for them. But I imagine that rich papa counted on running into some such extra expenses."

That seemed to be the story. But Maria had one more detail to add. "The wedding in the church down below was beautiful this morning," she said. "Lots of flowers, and everybody so dressed up. Naturally, the bride was crying. Especially as they came out of the church. Her father had hired a couple of men to stand outside the church door holding some balloons he'd had made, and as the bride and groom came out the men released the balloons. There were dozens of them, and the wind blew them all over the place, and lots of people grabbed them as souvenirs. Still, a great many of them flew straight up to Heaven, where they were meant to go. Because the bride's father had had something printed on the balloons. A message. Can you guess what it was?"

We got it of course, and Maria nodded. "Yes—'Ciao Fabrizio,'" she said. "Perhaps they didn't want to take a chance that he hadn't seen the fireworks from so far away."

Donald Hall
Lace and Onions 1956

THE STORM HELD OFF until after I had climbed to Isernia on the sloping end of a narrow plateau. The road wound around its edge and up to its far end, since the streets were too narrow for traffic to pass through the town; there, leaving the car in a little *piazza* outside the walls I walked through the medieval gateway. The main street was so steep and had so little width that the tall houses seemed to lean to meet overhead, and on either side yet narrower alleys turned off to trickle over the side of the plateau. There were few people about, but in most of the doorways women and girls sat making lace. One group set in a long, vaulted room open to the street was beautifully composed and I asked if I might take a photograph. The women nodded, smiling, and two of them put down their needles to tidy each other's hair, then went on with their work. When I had done, the girl by the doorway asked without looking up if I was an American, and, when I replied that I was English, said:

"We saw them in the war, but only the Americans took photographs. You must be an American."

As I went up the street a bunch of children began to chant *"Americano, Americano"*, dancing first on one foot then the other and doubling up with laughter when I pretended to drive them away. A carpenter in his open workshop who was watching hailed me and said it was a pity I had not come in June. That was the time, June 28th, when they had the fair of San Pietro dalle Cipolle. And what was notable about that, I asked. Why, the onions of course. People came from all over the world to see them; mounds of copper and wine-coloured onions of *notevole grandezza*, each one weighing at least a pound. Whey San Pietro, I inquired, what had he to do with onions? It had to do with the pope, Celestino V; his real name had been Pietro Angeleri and he had been born here at Isernia before going to Morrone near Sulmona where he had become a hermit. I said I knew about him, the pope of "the Great Refusal". In that case, he replied, looking a little disappointed, I probably knew the rest. I shook my head. Well, then, this Pietro was a very holy man who became so famous for his goodness that he was elected pope. But after five months he decided he was not worthy and resigned. Some said that Boniface VIII persuaded him because he had always wanted to be pope instead. It certainly looked like it because he shut up poor Pietro who soon died mysteriously. It was said that when the people of Isernia heard of this they cried and cried. So now they celebrate with onions? The carpenter laughed and asked if I should like some coffee, so we strolled up the street. Pietro died in May and the fair was in June, but dates get confused.

Mark Twain
A Common Miracle 1892

THE DOGS OF THE CAMPAGNA (they watch sheep without human assistance) are big and warlike, and are terrible creatures to meet in those lonely expanses. Two young Englishmen—one of them a friend of mine—were away out there yesterday, with a peasant guide of the region who is a simple-hearted and very devout Roman Catholic. At one point the guide stopped, and said they were now approaching a spot where two especially ferocious dogs were accustomed to herd sheep: that it would be well to go cautiously and be prepared to retreat if they saw the dogs. So then they started on, but presently came suddenly upon the dogs. The immense brutes came straight for them, with death in their eyes. The guide said in a voice of horror, "Turn your backs, but for God's sake don't stir—I will pray—I will pray the Virgin to do a miracle and save us; she will hear me, oh, my God she surely will." And straightway he began to pray. The Englishmen stood quaking with fright, and wholly without faith in the man's prayer. But all at once the furious snarling of the dogs ceased—at three steps distant—and there was dead silence. After a moment my friend, who could no longer endure the awful suspense, turned—and there was the miracle, sure enough: the gentleman dog had mounted the lady dog and both had forgotten their solemn duty in the ecstasy of a higher interest!

The strangers were saved, and they retired from that place with thankful hearts. The guide was in a frenzy of pious gratitude and exultation, and praised and glorified the Virgin without stint; and finally wound up with "But you—you are Protestants; she would not have done it for you; she did it for me—only me—praised be she for evermore! and I will hang a picture of it in the church and it shall be another proof that her loving care is still with her children who humbly believe and adore."

By the time the dogs got unattached the men were five miles from there.

Native customs are fine and dandy, but all we can do is watch. The best way to get to know Italians is to interact with them, to meet them in your travels, to buy things from them, to let them help you by giving directions. This is just what Emily Kimbrough, Edith Templeton, and Israeli humorist Ephraim Kishon did in the following pieces, with unexpected—or should-have-been-expected—consequences.

Emily Kimbrough
Associations 1954

WE STOPPED IN AREZZO briefly. We left the car in an open square in the upper section of the town and set out on foot to find Petrarch's house. We had come up the inevitable steep road that marks the approach to every hill town and had emerged on the inevitable square into which the approach empties. I was complaining a little as we started back down the hill on foot. I had been for days, I said, on a perpetual slant. If we explored many more hill towns I would present a very odd appearance by the time we reached England, something like the Tower of Pisa, walking. Furthermore, I was in a chronic condition of thinness of breath, what with the actual demands made on it when I was on foot, and my inner compulsion when in a car to hold it and at the same time push in order to get the Fiat and us to the summit.

I stopped my lament when I saw a man sunning in front of a little house. I asked him the way to the Petrarch Accademia. I had learned from Mr. Clark's guidebook that Petrarch's house was the headquarters of the Accademia.

Later, in the car as we moved on to Florence, Sophy harked back to this moment of my inquiry, using it as an example of my habitual involvement of the group in unwanted associations. It has been a long-standing contention between us developed through years of motor trips together. My subject for debate is that Sophy will never voluntarily ask directions of anyone, preferring either to wander or to sit in the car drawn up at the side of the road for what seems to me an interminable time, crouched over a map plastered against the steering wheel in front of her, as if she were in meditation before the Delphic Oracle awaiting a guiding sign from it. Simply to ask a passerby evidently humiliates both her and her oracle. I had not reminded her, I said, of this trait since the day we registered at the Berlitz School. Sophy's retort was her invariable counterattack that, if permitted, I would substitute passing travelers for mileposts and refer to them in the same frequency as the position of those landmarks, one to every mile, and that this procedure, since I am by nature loquacious, is not conducive to rapid progress. Furthermore, she is wont to point out, I sometimes take the milepost along with us, not always a particularly agreeable association.

Since the morning of May 16, the gentleman sunning himself in Arezzo has been one of her favorite examples of this sort of association. That gentleman, when I questioned him, leaped to his feet, pointed straight ahead of us in the direction in which we were already set—Sophy reminds me of this—and asked, "You Americans?"

I was the one who answered; the others moved ahead rapidly. "Yes," I said, "we are."

The man joined me at once and was with me when I caught up with my friends.

"I American, too," he told us all.

Sophy groaned and said to her companions, "You see what I mean?"

Their response was to close in with her and gang up against me. I felt it instantly.

The newcomer continued, "I from Chicago. Anybody know Chicago?"

I still think it would have been rude not to answer, though pressure has been brought to bear on me to admit this was where I made my greatest mistake.

"Yes," I said, "I know Chicago. I grew up there."

I thought for a moment the man would throw his arms around me and kiss me. He came perilously close, but stopped, his face pushed into mine, his arms wide. "Why I ever leave Chicago?" he demanded. "Tell me that. Chicago the most wonderful city in the world. You know the Loop?"

"Yes," I said, backing away a little. "I know it."

"You know wonderful store of Marshall Field?"

"Yes," I said, "I do. I worked there once."

With a deep sigh he lowered his arms, took my right hand in both his, causing my guidebook, notebook and sweater I was carrying under that arm, to fall to the ground. "Chicago is most beautiful city in whole world," he declared while we both endeavored to pick up the objects that had fallen, not an easy process since he continued to hold my hand in one of his. "Why am I such fool to leave most beautiful city in world?"

The others, once more, had moved on ahead of me. Sophy called back over her shoulder, "Don't tell him, I beg of you."

I compromised. "Well, why were you?" I asked. He released my hand and with both of his beat his breast.

"Because I think I am homesick for Italy. Because I am a fool. Because I do not know enough to stay where I am making good money, live good, raise my children good. No. What I do? I bring them all to Italy. I talk to them

183

years about Italy. I want them to see where papa grow up, papa's old friends. We come. And what happen? Friends have forgot papa. I have forgot them. Children no like it. Wife no like it. I no like it anymore. So what happens?"

We had caught up with the others standing in front of Petrarch's house. Sophy spoke briefly to me. "It wasn't very difficult to find," she said, and turned to the others. "Do we want to go on with this," she asked, "and hear all about Chicago, or should we give up the whole thing and go on to Florence?

They decided to go to Florence. No one asked me to vote. We turned, and like the King of France, marched right up the hill again.

My companion was momentarily put off in his narrative. "You no want to see this place?"

"My friends think we must be on our way," I explained.

"Okay," he agreed cheerfully, and turned back with me. "Nothing much to see anyway. Very old. Everything in Italy, very old. Too old. Not new like Chicago."

"Well, why don't you go back to Chicago?" I asked, and began as usual to wheeze a little as the grade became steeper.

My wandering minstrel stopped in the road, flinging out his arms again. "Why I not go back?" he repeated dramatically. "You ask me that. Because in this dumb country, I no make enough money to get us all back again."

I had not stopped with him. I was endeavoring to keep up with my friends.

He hurried after me. "Maybe I work for you?" he suggested.

I heard a deep groan from Sophy ahead of us.

"Because you love Chicago," he continued. "I work hard, and one day I bring my family back. We all work for you. See Chicago. See the Loop again."

We had reached the car. The others were already in it and Sophy put her foot on the starter. I jumped in and closed the door quickly after me.

The Chicagoan looked wistfully into the back seat, but I held the door firmly. The window was down and I spoke through it. "No," I said, "I can't take you."

Zella addressed the other three. "Well," she said, "we can be glad of that, anyway."

I had opened my purse, relinquishing for a moment my hold on the door, and from a compartment that held a small fund for emergencies, I drew a dollar bill. I counted this an emergency. "Here is something," I said, "to remind you of America," and handed it to him.

The car began to move away from him. He was holding the dollar bill between his hands and was kissing it. "Don't forget," I called back to him, "you didn't like it when you were there. I think it's lovely here."

He checked a kiss on its way to the bill. "Bah," he said. "Here I spit," and illustrated on the ground. "Here I kiss," and completed the salute to the American dollar.

We drove off. There was no conversation among us as we descended the hill, but when we came out of the town and into the countryside again, Sophy asked courteously, "Well, now that we haven't seen Arezzo, would you like to tell us about the Loop?"

Ephraim Kishon
Full of Benevolence 1957

IT IS ONLY NATURAL THAT THE TOURIST should like the charming and cheerful Italians. But that the Italians, too, should like tourists borders on perversion. It almost looks as if the Italians were out to disprove Lipshitz's dictum on the despicable globe-trotter: they see in the tourist a human being and treat him with affectionate benevolence. Sometimes they are so benevolent that one simply does not understand what's going on.

Take for instance reticent Luigi.

I ran into him in Genoa, the day after my arrival. After wandering around in the city's mazelike alleys, I found I had completely lost my way. I therefore walked up to some people waiting for the bus not far from the port, and asked a rubicund elderly gentleman carrying a small parcel in his hands, where was the Excelsior Hotel. My marvellous instinct had again proved itself: the man spoke tolerably good German.

"Excelsior Hotel? Come," he said simply. We boarded the bus and sat down next to each other. My volunteer guide pointed to the parcel he was carrying and explained:

"I bought myself some woollen drawers."

"Yes," I said, "really?"

"I need to have something warm round my belly in winter," the gentleman continued, "otherwise I'll catch a cold. My wife always says to me: 'Don't be ashamed, Luigi, tie a Turkish towel under your pants'. That is, she knows that I'm a little bashful. We fight a great deal because of that. She, for instance, always hangs her bras and slips to dry out on the porch. I've told her a hundred times if I've told her once: 'Do you want to become the talk of the whole neighbourhood?' So she answers back: 'Better take care of yourself and stop coming home every night dead drunk'. Did you hear that, sir? She has the nerve to talk like that when she's so fat the chairs are collapsing under her."

"Well yes," I answered, "such is life."

"I married her without a penny to her name," Luigi informed me. "She didn't bring as much as a rag into the marriage, but about that she chooses to keep mum. All she knows is nag, nag, nag! And she's jealous, Madonna of Padua help her, she's insanely jealous. For years she's suspected me of carrying on with Signora Catini who has a news-stand next to the Cathedral, there on the right side of the arcades. And I swear, sir, that she, my wife that is, looks much better than the Catini woman, and to this day makes my sap rise much faster—though she is getting fat. But you can't talk sense to her, she's a madwoman. It's always Signora Catini this, Signora Catini that, every night she whines, 'you again bought your paper from her, I saw it with my own eyes'. So what, can't I buy my paper from Signora Catini? Tell me, sir, is that a crime?"

"No," I mumbled, "why should it be a crime?"

Our bus was now running along the seashore. The scenery was breathtaking. But there was no sign of the Excelsior Hotel I was looking for.

"The only thing she and her mother know is to cackle all day long," Luigi went on describing his predicament. "More than once I asked them: 'for the sake of the Madonna of Padua, how can you talk so much?' You know what the old woman answered? 'Shut up your big mouth', she said to me, so help me, 'you and your criminal record!' That is, once, about two and a half years ago, they locked me up for a while because we had drunk a little, me and Marcello, and were in high spirits, and tossed some potted plants from the public garden through a few house windows, but even the judge said: 'Luigi,' he said, 'I'll take into consideration your blameless past and also your bitter fate'. Now I'm asking you, sir, can you call that a criminal record? If you must know it, she comes from one of those families, only I don't like to speak about it. Her dad was a smuggler, of narcotics, they say, it's no secret, everyone will tell you, he had three fingers shot off on one hand. Once my little daughter came home from school and asked me: 'Daddy, is it true that they had hanged grandad?' What should I have told her? Do I have to lie to the child, isn't it bad enough that she fails every year at school? I said to her, 'child, I got to get off here'."

With that Luigi got up and prepared to get off the bus which had just then stopped.

187

"Pardon me," I said, "is it much longer to the Hotel Excelsior?"

"Couldn't tell you, never heard this name," Luigi replied cheerfully. "But we had a good chat, hadn't we? I live here. Good luck, sir."

Edith Templeton
Transacting a Tarantula c1957

IN THE MORNING I GO TO CHANGE a traveller's cheque. The bank is part of that modern block running alongside the whole length of the public gardens, called the Galleria, no doubt after the Galleria in Milan; but in this case the glass-roofed street inside the house does not form a cross, but cuts diagonally from one corner of the building to the corner opposite. The Galleria in Milan is a monster, with a monster's grandeur, inspired by the same love for vaulted glass roofs which called into being the Crystal Palace and Victoria Station. But the Galleria of Cremona is of quite recent date, and lacks the generosity of the nineteenth century. Upon entering it I feel that I have been swallowed up by a whale, and shall come out mangled by all those shopkeepers who stand grinning in front of their shops in the milky light beneath the glass vault.

I enter, present my cheque, and a shiver runs through the bank. Various gentlemen leave their counters to peer over the shoulder of the clerk who is holding the paper. Doors at the back open and there come forth other gentlemen who, during a normal banking day, were never meant to be revealed.

I hand in my passport, and now the two documents are being carried about from one table to the other, from one counter to the other, by men with panic-stricken features.

"You have it."

"No, you give it to him."

"No, he doesn't want it."

"Here you are, you'd better deal with it."

"I've had it once already, you fool, what am I to do with it?"

And this is the bank which has a notice in the window saying that foreign business will gladly be transacted. They transact it as gladly as handling a tarantula spider.

In the end, ironically enough, it is the youngest of the clerks who grasps the tarantula. He digs out some printed forms, fills them in, and tears them up once they have been written. This is a well-known creative process known by writers as "warming up". At last he is satisfied with his work. He hands it to the others, who now are very knowledgeable. The layout is criticized and amended. The end is near.

I am given a metal disk with a number stamped on it, sign the cheque, and go to the cashier's grille. While he pays me, my passport does yet another round from hand to hand, a sort of farewell visit. By now, all the bank knows my age, and I have a horrible feeling that, later on, they will tell each other how old they thought I was and how far they were off the mark. For all I know they may already have established one of their colleagues, with a book, accepting bets.

"For God's sake, Malcolm, can't you forget the
Dow Jones Average for one day?"

Serrano

ᶿTourists

ᶿ*Although you may go to Italy thinking you'll meet Italians and find out what sort of people they really are, you will most likely find yourself meeting more tourists than natives, many of them, however, just as interesting as the natives. You stay in the same hotels, visit the same sites, and take the same trains. You are also more likely to speak the same language. After attempting to order lunch in a village* caffè, *the lilt of a voice from outermost Scotland might seem down-home to a Mississippian, and vice versa (please excuse my classic Italian).*

Italians are definitely full of humorous possibilities, but it is the tourist who is the true humorist's favorite subject, and object (known in some parts as "the butt"). The Italian in Italy knows exactly what he's about, who he is and why he's doing what he's doing, that is, living off the tourist. The tourist in Italy, especially the tourist who is traveling with others but not on a tour, is conflicted, both internally and externally. In other words, he wants to do everything and she wants to do everything, but their everythings are rarely the same. So they compromise on doing a few things, most of which the entire party would rather pass up. Out of conflict humor blossoms like weeds from between the stones of a patio.

Here are a few choice dandelions from an unusual variety of writers who took and take glee in laughing at their fellows, that is, at us. First, Aubrey Menen tells us how the tourist can become simpatico, *the gold medal of Italian touristing. Then such writers as novelists William*

*Dean Howells and Charles Dickens, poet Harlan Hoge
Ballard, travel writers John Gibbons, Tibor Koeves, and,
of course, George Mikes, tell us all we need to know about
the tourist in Italy.*

Aubrey Menen
Becoming Simpatico 1962

A T FIRST, THE FOREIGNER finds it easy to live in
Italy. This is because the Italians ignore him completely. From long experience, they know that there is
nothing else to do with him. Every foreigner goes
through a stage when he regards the beauties of the
country, its sometimes ideal climate, its monuments and
its hundred other delights as being made specially for his
entertainment. He treats the country like his private Luna
Park. The Italians see to it that there are plenty of booths
and plenty of attendants to take his money off him, and
they leave it at that. This is known as tourism, and is
Italy's biggest industry. Tourism was invented by
tourists, who, when they do not get it, demand it vehe-
mently. The Italians, to oblige them, have set up a string
of hotels in places where tourists want them. They are
called Jolly Hotels. In Italian, Jolly means the card in the
pack which we call the Joker.

When the foreigner has lived in Italy long enough to
put off his cap and bells and when he has learned a little
of the language, the Italians will begin, cautiously, to talk
to him. If he behaves himself as though he were in his
own country—that is to say, if he obeys the laws, remem-
bers his manners and minds his own business—he will
one day hear himself called *"simpatico."*

For the English-speaking foreigners (and for the
Frenchman, too) this is a most dangerous word. It sounds
very like "sympathetic." The foreigner who thinks that the
Italians find him sympathetic should remember that the

Italians have been invaded and, in some cases, conquered by the Berbers, the Arabs, the Greeks, the Germans, the French, the Austrians, and Spaniards, the Americans and the British, with the aid-in-arms of the Indians, the American Negroes, the Senegalese, the Somalis, the Australians, the New Zealanders and some others that I do not remember, but whom the Italians never forget. It is true that the Italian bears little resentment for being so variously disemboweled, stabbed, speared, bayonetted, burned, looted, machine-gunned, shelled and bombed. But he does not find it sympathetic, even in retrospect. The word *simpatico* merely means that the foreigner does not set his teeth on edge.

But if the foreigner is not *simpatico*, the Italians have had centuries of experience in knowing how to deal with him. If the foreigner challenges them, in the end he will lose. The end has come: the foreigner has lost completely.

Charles Dickens
Italian Dressings 1844

I THINK THE MOST POPULAR and most crowded sight (excepting those of Easter Sunday and Monday, which are open to all classes of people) was the Pope washing the feet of Thirteen men, representing the twelve apostles and Judas Iscariot. * * *

The body of the room was full of male strangers; the crowd immense; the heat very great; and the pressure sometimes frightful. It was at its height when the stream came pouring in, from the feet-washing; and then there were such shrieks and outcries that a party of Piedmontese dragoons went to the rescue of the Swiss Guard, and helped them to calm the tumult.

The ladies were particularly ferocious in their struggles for places. One lady of my acquaintance was seized round the waist, in the ladies' box, by a strong matron, and hoisted out of her place; and there was another lady (in a back row in the same box) who improved her position by sticking a large pin into the ladies before her.

The gentlemen about me were remarkably anxious to see what was on the table; and one Englishman seemed to have embarked the whole energy of his nature in the determination to discover whether there was any mustard. "By Jupiter there's vinegar!" I heard him say to his friend, after he had stood on tiptoe an immense time, and had been crushed and beaten on all sides. "And there's oil!! I saw them distinctly, in cruets! Can any gentleman, in front there, see mustard on the table? Sir, will you oblige me! Do you see a mustard-pot?"

John Gibbons
Our Own People Abroad 1932

IN NAPLES AND ROME and the cities, everybody of that class had the manners of princes and princesses. Which was more than could be said of our own people abroad. For the English that I met in Italy had manners about as bad as could well have been imagined. There was one instance that I especially remember for its curious contrast. A station refreshment-room somewhere in the middle of the night it was, and though I was not going by train myself, I had dropped in for a drink. There was an English lady there, and I suppose that she was off one of the international trains and was waiting for a connection, and she had a handful of rather measly-looking and faded flowers, which she handed to the very splendid head-waiter with the air of a mediæval princess bestowing largesse on a favoured slave. The *"Grazzia, Signora"* and the bow with which he received the offering were nothing less than magnificent, and one felt that the favour was inestimable. Now if she had spoken in

English, I believe it would have been all right, but of course she had to air her three-ha'pennyworth of bad French, and of course the man did not understand her. So that when, a quarter of an hour later, she demanded the flowers back again, and it came out that all she had really wanted was to have the beastly things put in water, it came as a bit of a surprise, but the *"Grazzia"* and the bow were again wonderful. But the very best bow of all, I think, came when the lady, having made her regal departure, the waiter turned round to the two or three Italians in the place and with a simply marvellous *"Grazzia,"* held up the equivalent of about half a farthing. And we were always doing it. Only the Americans, thank Heaven, were worse still.

There was one Cathedral I went to, and I was kneeling on the stone floor with quite a lot more people. And entirely regardless of the Service, there came along an American lady with a large and gorgeously-covered guide-book and a small and rather sober-coloured husband. She was identifying in her book this and that famous carving and altar-painting, and taking good care that her miserable spouse identified them too. And then, her pious task completed, she was just leaving the sacred building, when it occurred to her to identify us as well, the deluded and ignorant peasantry bowing down as no doubt we worshipped our stocks and stones. "Say, and aren't some people simply wonderful?" she put it to her bored husband, and "They are indeed, Madam. And will you kindly stop waving your umbrella at me?" came from an unknown voice somewhere in the middle of the worshippers.

And as of course it had never dawned upon the poor woman that anyone for hundreds of miles round could possibly speak English, I am convinced that she thought a new miracle had somehow occurred.

William Dean Howells
Pleasant Illusions 1908

"SHALL I NOT TAKE MINE EASE in mine inn?" the traveller asks rather anxiously than defiantly when he finds himself a stranger in a strange place, and he is apt to add, if he has not written or wired ahead to some specific hotel, "Which of mine inns shall I take mine ease in?" He is the more puzzled to choose the more inns there are to choose from, and his difficulty is enhanced if he has not considered that some of his inns may be full or may be too dear, and yet others undesirable.

The run from Naples in four hours and a half had been so flattering fair an experience to people who had last made it in eight that they arrived in Rome on a sunny afternoon of January preoccupied with expectations of an instant ease in their inn which seemed the measure of their merit. They indeed found their inn, and it was with a painful surprise that they did not find the rooms in it which they wanted. There were neither rooms full south, nor over the garden, nor off the tram, and in these circumstances there was nothing for it but to drive to some one else's inn and try for better quarters there. They, in fact, drove to half a dozen such, their demands rising for more rooms and sunnier and quieter and cheaper, the fewer and darker and noisier and dearer were those they found.

The trouble was that they found in the very first alien hotel where they applied an apartment so exactly what they wanted, with its four rooms and bath, all more or less full south, though mostly veering west and north, that they carried the fatal norm in their consciousness and tested all other apartments by it, the earlier notion of single rooms being promptly rejected after the sight of it. The reader will therefore not be so much astonished as these travellers were to learn that there was nothing else in Rome (where there must be about five hundred hotels, *hôtels garnis*, and pensions) that one could comparatively stay even overnight in, and that they settled in that alluring apartment provisionally, the next day being Sunday, and the crystalline Saturday of their arrival being well worn away toward its topaz and ruby sunset. Of course, they continued their search for several days afterward, zealously but hopelessly, yet not fruitlessly, for it resulted in an acquaintance with Roman hotels which they might otherwise never have made and, for one of them, in literary material of interest to every one hoping to come to Rome or despairing of it. The psychology of the matter was very curious, and involved the sort of pleasing self-illusion by which people so often get themselves over questionable passes in life and come out with a good conscience, or a dead one, which is practically the same thing. These particular people had come to Rome with reminiscences of inexpensiveness and had intended to recoup themselves for the cost of several previous winters in New York hotels by the saving they would make in their Roman sojourn. When it appeared, after all the negotiation and consequent abatement, that their Roman hotel apartment would cost them hardly a fifth less than they had last paid in New York, they took a guilty refuge in the fact that they were getting for less money something which no money could buy in New York. Gradually all sense of guilt wore off, and they boldly, or even impudently, said to themselves that they ought to have what they could pay for, and that there were reasons, which they were not obliged to render in their frankest soliloquies, why they should do just what they chose in the matter.

Harlan Hoge Ballard
In the Catacombs c1890

Sam Brown was a fellow from way down East,
Who never was "staggered" in the least.
No tale of marvellous beast or bird
Could match the stories he had heard;
No curious place or wondrous view
"Was ekil to Podunk, I tell yu."

If they told him of Italy's sunny clime,
"Maine kin beat it, every time!"
If they marvelled at
Etna's fount of fire,
They roused his ire:
With an injured air
He'd reply, "I swear
I don't think much of a smokin' hill;
We've got a moderate little rill
Kin make yer old volcaner still:
Jes' pour old Kennebec down the crater,
'N' I guess it'll cool her fiery nater!"

They showed him a room where a queen had
        slept;
"'T'wan't up to the tavern daddy kept."
They showed him Lucerne; but he had drunk
From the beautiful Molechunkamunk.
They took him at last to ancient Rome,
And inveigled him into a catacomb:

Here they plied him with draughts of wine,
Though he vowed old cider was twice as fine,
Till the fumes of Falernian filled his head,
And he slept as sound as the silent dead.

They removed a mummy to make him room,
And laid him at length in the rocky tomb.

They piled old skeletons round the stone,
Set a "dip" in a candlestick of bone,
And left him to slumber there alone
Then watched from a distance the taper's gleam,
Waiting to jeer at his frightened scream,
When he should wake from his drunken dream.

After a time the Yankee woke,
But instantly saw through the flimsy joke;
So never a cry or shout he uttered,
But solemnly rose, and slowly muttered:
"I see how it is. It's the judgment day,
We've all been dead and stowed away;
All these stone furreners sleepin' yet,
An' I'm the fust one up, you bet!
Can't none o' you Romans start, I wonder?
United States ahead, by thunder!"

Tibor Koeves
In the Know 1939

DON'T LIKE "INSIDERS!" My first encounter with the type occurred in Venice. The man in question was my compatriot, an artist, who lost no time assuring me he knew every stone and every pretty girl in the city. He wore corduroy trousers, sandals, and a shirt open at the collar; hearing that I had just arrived, he grasped my arm and offered to show me around.

Right at the start we ran into three urchins, loudly inveighing against each other. My friend leaned against the wall and shook with laughter.

"You wouldn't understand," he hissed, breathless with mirth; "you have no idea how picturesque the Venetian lingo is!"

At the next corner he stepped up to a passerby, whispered in his ear, winked at him, and came back.

"It's not so easy," he remarked thoughtfully; "I guess I can take care of it, though," he added, smiling, with a shrug of his shoulder, while it remained for me to appreciate the importance of whatever it was he had tried to arrange.

At dinner-time he took a long way around to a dirty little restaurant. "No foreigners come here," he observed; "it's the best place in town, and they're having gnocchi for dinner today."

So saying he went out to the kitchen, ordered his food straight from the cook, and pinched the snub nose of the one and only waitress. The gnocchi were hard and stale, but my friend honored me by awarding me the check.

After dinner he deluged me with information. He knew just where to buy cheap smuggled wine, who was whose mistress, and where to dispose of old hats. I remarked I was dying to get a dozen coffin nails, and then and there he gave me the name of a reliable firm, without a moment's hesitation.

Paddling past the Ca d'Oro, he shoved me in the ribs.

"The Ca d'Oro," he whispered, as if to point out a rare jungle beast I should never have spotted but for his scent. Then he launched into a lecture on Venetian history, but got all his dates wrong.

When he came to Saint Mark's Place, he stopped and looked me in the eye. "How do you like it?" his eyes were asking me, as he took me by the hand, and led me on tiptoe beneath the central cupola. There he let my hand go, took a deep breath, and threw his arms wide open.

"There!" he sighed.

His voice trembled, his eyes were ecstatic, while his cheeks shone with a preternatural pride. Some demon possessed me as I saw him standing there arms akimbo, and throwing my arms about him, I kissed him cere-

moniously on both cheeks. "You are a great artist," I
assured him. "Your work will live forever."

Blushing, he lowered his eyes.

"You wouldn't spoof me," he demurred. But I could tell
by his tone he considered the praise niggardly.

Charles Dickens
The Davises 1844

AVAILING OURSELVES of a part of the quiet inter-
val between the termination of the Carnival and
the beginning of the Holy Week, when everybody had
run away from the one, and few people had yet begun to
run back again for the other, we went conscientiously to
work, to see Rome. And, by dint of going out early every
morning, and coming back late every evening, and
labouring hard all day, I believe we made acquaintance
with every post and pillar in the city, and the country
round; and in particular explored so many churches that
I abandoned that part of the enterprise at last, before it
was half finished, lest I should never, of my own accord,
go to church again, as long as I lived. But I managed,
almost every day, at one time or other, to get back to the
Colosseum, and out upon the open Campagna, beyond
the Tomb of Cecilia Metella.

We often encountered, in these expeditions, a company of English Tourists, with whom I had an ardent, but
ungratified longing to establish a speaking acquaintance.
They were one Mr. Davis, and a small circle of friends. It
was impossible not to know Mrs. Davis's name, from her
being always in great request among her party, and her
party being everywhere. During the Holy Week, they
were in every part of every scene of every ceremony. For
a fortnight or three weeks before it, they were in every
tomb, and every church, and every ruin, and every Picture Gallery; and I hardly ever observed Mrs. Davis to be

silent for a moment. Deep underground, high up in St. Peter's, out on the Campagna, and stifling in the Jews' quarter, Mrs. Davis turned up, all the same. I don't think she ever saw anything, or ever looked at anything; and she had always lost something out of a straw hand-basket, and was trying to find it, with all her might and main, among an immense quantity of English halfpence, which lay, like sands upon the seashore, at the bottom of it. There was a professional *cicerone* always attached to the party (which had been brought over from London, fifteen or twenty strong, by contract), and if he so much as looked at Mrs. Davis, she invariably cut him short by saying, "There, God bless the man, don't worrit me! I don't understand a word you say, and shouldn't if you was to talk till you was black in the face!" Mr. Davis always had a snuff-coloured great-coat on, and carried a great green umbrella in his hand, and had a slow curiosity constantly devouring him, which prompted him to do extraordinary things, such as taking the covers off urns in tombs, and looking in at the ashes as if they were pickles—and tracing out inscriptions with the ferrule of his umbrella, and saying, with intense thoughtfulness, "Here's a B, you see, and there's a R, and this is the way we goes on in; is it!" His antiquarian habits occasioned his being frequently in the rear of the rest; and one of the agonies of Mrs. Davis, and the party in general, was an ever-present fear that Davis would be lost. This caused them to scream for him, in the strangest places, and at the most improper seasons. And when he came, slowly emerging out of some sepulchre or other, like a peaceful Ghoul, saying, "Here I am!" Mrs. Davis invariably replied, "You'll be buried alive in a foreign country, Davis, and it's no use trying to prevent you!"

Mr. and Mrs. Davis, and their party, had, probably, been brought from London in about nine or ten days. Eighteen hundred years ago, the Roman legions under Claudius protested against being led into Mr. and Mrs.

Davis's country, urging that it lay beyond the limits of the world.

George Mikes
A Great Natural Resource 1956

THE POSITION OF THE TOURISTS in Italy is unique because they have made a strong impact on the natives. The Italians would not be what they are without the tourists.

Other countries have coal or oil or gold. Italy has tourists. Of course, other countries, too, have foreign visitors but in Italy the tourists represent natural resources. Tourists are the greatest single blessing bestowed by nature on the land.

Tourists possess a number of advantages over coal or oil. On the whole they are cleaner than coal. Tourists, like coal, cause a number of problems of transportation but, unlike coal, they pay their own fares. Then, atomic energy may one day replace coal and oil, but while it may do a great many things with tourists, too, it will never replace them.

It is an arguable point whether it is more difficult to exploit coal-mines than to exploit tourists but, in any case, the two processes require different techniques.

What is the psychological influence of the crowds—the endless legions—of tourists invading Italy? Naturally enough, they raise Italian self-admiration (never very low) to a higher pitch. They also create the impression that tourists are incredibly silly—just mugs, to employ an old Roman expression. First the Italian inhabitants of, let us say, Positano, find it flattering that people from every Continent—literally from all over the world—flock to their small village to drink in its breathtaking and improbable beauty. They feel rather like the British aristocracy who open their homes to the public. But the British peer can stand at the turnstile and insist on every visitor dropping half-a-crown or a little more into his top-hat. Italian fishermen would never stoop so low as to charge an entrance fee to Positano. So they have to resort to other ways and means to charm cash out of the tourists' pockets (ways and means not altogether unfamiliar to our nobility either).

The fisherman in common with the other Italians think tourists silly to undertake long journeys across Oceans and Continents just to see what is (for them) just right there all the time. They are fully aware of the beauty of their village and their country. Yet it seems an odd whim that people should travel thousands of miles to see those familiar sights. And while the tourists only see the azure skies, the blue sea, the quaint church, the gay little shops, the steep and narrow streets and the lovely terraced houses which look as if they were just about to fall into the sea—the natives also know the inside of these houses. They also know that the tourist season is followed by winter. They wonder if all these foreigners have come to Positano to admire their poverty or their riches. It is natural for people—they feel instinctively—to be willing to pay an entrance fee to gain admittance to a more opulent and luxuriant world. But to see something dull and shabby? Should the Dukes of Marlborough and Norfolk ask my permission to come and visit my flat and offer me 5/- (2/6d. each, I mean) I should probably lead them through all my four rooms and recount the history of our settee and our drinking cabinet, but their desire to see my flat would not heighten my respect for their Graces. The Italian fishermen, I am convinced, follow the same train of thought.

There is a further decisive difference between coal and the tourist. Coal stays where it is unless the mine is exploited with great skill and hard work. The tourist, on the other hand, goes away in no time whether he is or is not exploited with great skill and hard labour. The tourist is a temporary—fleeting—phenomenon and every lira he takes away with him is a measure of his host's failure and a dead loss.

There is nothing nasty in this mentality. When I speak of tourists as the natural resources of Italy I am not trying to pull off a facile paradox. I am being faithful to reality. Tourists are regarded as God's gift; as manna from Heaven; as a challenge to people's ingenuity to make the most of them. You cannot blame British miners for working too slowly and, at the same time, blame the Italian diggers for making short shrift of tourists; you simply cannot have it both ways.

While the majority of the Italians have nothing to do directly with tourists, this mentality is infectious. Women they want to conquer at lightning speed; in business they want to grow rich in no time. They are in the habit of regarding all opportunities as bulls, taking them by the horns and milking them with impatient vigour.

You may object that one cannot milk bulls. The Italians try. And it would surprise you to find how often they succeed.

Exhausted, sunburnt, broke, and headed for a good long diet, you finally go home. You wonder if you will ever feel romantic again, if you can ever look at another noodle or sausage, if your rear will ever lose those pinchmarks. You worry that your friends will assure you you've missed all the best towns, hotels, and restaurants, or that you don't understand Michelangelo at all. And will your gifts be enough to satisfy those you left behind?

Don't worry. You can't satisfy anyone any of the time, so feel satisfied yourself. Or repeat to yourself the following poem by the king of nonsense, Edward Lear.

Edward Lear
Says I to Myself c1845

Says I to myself
glad I shall be,
when I am free,
O Rome from thee,
& over the sea,
high diddledydee.

That's it. Completamente. *It's time to say* ciao, arrivederci, buon viaggio, *and to get ready to take the plunge. You should be prepared now for the best and the worst, for the strangest and the most ordinary and familiar. You shouldn't fall into any traps or, for that matter, trap anyone yourself. But don't let your trip be uneventful, and if you've gone to Italy already, don't let your memories be uneventful. In any, and all events, enjoy!*

"It's a little something we brought back from Venice."

Acknowledgments

ROY BLOUNT, JR.: From *Now, Where Were We* by Roy Blount, Jr., Copyright © 1988 by Roy Blount, Jr. Reprinted by permission of the author and Villard Books, a Division of Random House, Inc. ALAN BRIEN: Reproduced by permission of *Punch*. ART BUCHWALD: Reprinted with the kind permission of the author. KAREL CAPEK: Translated by Francis P. Marchant and edited by the editor. ALAN COREN: Reproduced by permision of *Punch*. E. M. FORSTER: Reprinted from *A Room with a View* by E. M. Forster. Published 1923 by Alfred A. Knopf, Inc. Reprinted by permission of the publisher. JOHN GIBBONS: From *Afoot in Italy* by John Gibbons. Copyright 1932 by E.P. Dutton, renewed 1959 by John Gibbons. Reprinted by permission of the publisher, E.P. Dutton, a divison of NAL Penguin Inc. RUBE GOLDBERG AND SAM BOAL: Reprinted from *Rube Goldberg's Guide to Europe* by Rube Goldberg and Sam Boal by permission of the publisher, Vanguard Press, Inc., a division of Random House, Inc. Copyright © 1954 by Rube Goldberg and Sam Boal. Renewed © 1982 by Irma Goldberg and Sam Boal. HALDANE: Reproduced by permission of *Punch*. DONALD HALL: Reprinted from *Eagle Argent* by Donald Hall, Methuen & Co., © 1956 Donald Hall, by permission of the publisher. MERRILY HARPUR: Reproduced by permission of *Punch*. IRENE KAMPEN: Reprinted by permission of International Creative Management, Inc. Copyright © 1965 by Irene Kampen. EMILY KIMBROUGH: Reprinted from *Forty Plus and Fancy Free*, Harper Bros., © 1954 Emily Kimbrough, by the kind permission of the author. EPHRAIM KISHON: Reprinted from *The Seasick Whale*, André Deutsch, 1965, trans. from the Hebrew by Yohanan Goldman, by permission of Eric Glass Ltd. TIBOR KOEVES: From *Timetable for Tramps* by Tibor Koeves. Copyright © 1939 by Tibor Koeves. Copyright © renewed 1967 by Tibor Koeves. Reprinted by permission of Houghton Mifflin Company. ANATOL KOVARSKY: Reprinted from *Kovarsky's World*, Knopf, © 1956 Anatol Kovarsky, by the kind permission of the artist. STEPHEN LONGSTREET: Reprinted from *Last Man Around the*

THE HUMORISTS' GUIDES

THE HUMORISTS' GUIDES are available in better book-stores everywhere. Or, order directly by mail. Send a check or money order for $9.95 per book, plus $1.50 for shipping, no matter how many books you order (in Canada, $2.50; NJ residents only, add sales tax of 6% (60¢ per book)).

If you would like to receive information about future Cat-bird books, please send us your name and address on this form or any other way you choose. Please send orders and names to: *Catbird Press, 44 North Sixth Avenue, Highland Park, NJ 08904*. Or call 201-572-0816, 9-5 Eastern time.

No. of
<u>copies</u>

Savoir Rire: The Humorists' Guide to France
When in Rome: The Humorists' Guide to Italy
In a Fog: The Humorists' Guide to England
All in the Same Boat: The Humorists' Guide
to the Ocean Cruise

Total Number of Copies   x $9.95 = _____

Plus shipping ($1.50; Can. $2.50)   _____

Plus sales tax (NJ only)   x $ .60 = _____

Total enclosed   _____

Name_____

Address_____

City _____ State _____ Zip _____

Ship to, if different:

Name_____

Address_____

City _____ State _____ Zip _____

THE HUMORISTS' GUIDES

THE HUMORISTS' GUIDES are available in better book-stores everywhere. Or, order directly by mail. Send a check or money order for $9.95 per book, plus $1.50 for shipping, no matter how many books you order (in Canada, $2.50; NJ residents only, add sales tax of 6% (60¢ per book)).

If you would like to receive information about future Catbird books, please send us your name and address on this form or any other way you choose. Please send orders and names to: *Catbird Press, 44 North Sixth Avenue, Highland Park, NJ 08904.* Or call 201-572-0816, 9-5 Eastern time.

No. of
<u>copies</u>

Savoir Rire: The Humorists' Guide to France
When in Rome: The Humorists' Guide to Italy
In a Fog: The Humorists' Guide to England
All in the Same Boat: The Humorists' Guide
to the Ocean Cruise

Total Number of Copies   x $9.95 = _____

Plus shipping ($1.50; Can. $2.50)   _____

Plus sales tax (NJ only)   x $ .60 = _____

Total enclosed   _____

Name_____

Address_____

City _____ State _____ Zip _____

Ship to, if different:

Name_____

Address_____

City _____ State _____ Zip _____